U0069383

玳瑚師父 著
Master Dai Hu

向善向上 2

Towards Kindness,
Towards Betterment 2

序

沒有沒有用的人

舉凡是人，大致上都不喜被冠上三個字。哪三個字？即「沒有用」也。

其實啊！吾，玳瑚師父，學佛開啟了智慧後，妙觀這世間眾生，都有她他們一定的用處，根本就沒有沒有用的人。唯存的是，妳你或她他，到底有沒有盡心盡力、全力以赴的去完成每一件事兒。若答案是有的話，那妳你與她他又怎能歸類於「沒有用的人」呢？

當然！若妳你不介意被冠上「沒有用」這三個字的話，那就請便。不過吾還是勸妳你，三思再三思。因為，妳你未來的後代，肯定會出現沒有用的子女哦！到時妳你拼命叫，或教她他有用，很難很難會如妳你所願。為什麼？因果也。

記住玳瑚師父的話，根本就沒有沒有用的人，而是妳你到底有沒有發揮妳你最大的潛能。大家一起來做個最有用的人，造福自己，造福一切眾生，圓滿我們這一生。

善書多閱，好運增上。

There Ain't No Useless Person

Most people usually will not like to be labelled this word. Which word is that? The word - Useless.

Actually, after increased wisdom from learning the Dharma, I have observed that every sentient being in this world has his or her own strengths to contribute. Therefore, there is no such thing as a totally useless person. Rather, it is a question of diligence and sincerity, and whether he or she gives his/her best effort to complete a task. If these qualities are exemplified in abundance, how can you fall into the category of a useless person?

Of course, if you do not mind being labelled as such, then please go ahead by all means. However, I will advise you to reconsider such notion because your descendants will surely take after you and your uselessness! When this happens, it is futile even if you shout with all your might, or exhaust your entire life to right the wrong. Why? Karmic retribution.

Do remember these words from Master Dai Hu. There is no useless person, only one who has yet to uncover the greatest potential in him or her. Let us do our part and be a useful person, to create benefits for ourselves and all sentient beings, accomplishing the very essence of our life here on Earth.

Read more virtuous books and watch your good fortune soar.

個人網址 Website：www.masterdaihu.com
臉書專頁 Facebook page：www.facebook.com/masterdaihu
聯絡號碼 Contact number：+65 90284291

目　錄
CONTENTS

純真的愛 Pure Love

當初你們親密時，難道他有拿槍逼妳嗎？
When you shared intimate moments,did he use a gun to force you?

可是…
But...
您看他那個樣子！
look at his attitude!

怎麼現在妳就變成母夜叉，還請人幫妳下降頭呢？
Why do you turn into an evil demoness now, wanting to hire a sorcerer to cast malevolent spells onto him?

我愛他啊！
I love him!
他怎麼可以這樣對我？
How can he treat me like this?

那根本不是愛，是恨。
That is not love at all. It's hatred.

妳跟有婦之夫在一起，本來就是錯。孔子說：「己所不欲，勿施於人。」

You were wrong in the first place to start a relationship with a married man.
Confucius said, "One should not impose on others what he himself does not desire."

妳如果不要人家來破壞妳的家庭，妳也不要去破壞別人的家庭。

If you do not wish for your family to be broken, do not break up another person's family.

更不要去做別人的小三、小四、小五。

Don't be a 3rd, 4th or 5th party to another relationship.

快醒醒！
這是一種惡行！
Wake up, wake up quickly!

不能用法術去對付不懂法術的人。
This is an evil act. You cannot use spells on a person with no such skills.

是他先傷害我的！
他怎麼可以背叛我的愛！
He hurt me first!
How can he betray my love!

拿妳錢的降頭師，將來也一定會有禍害。
The sorcerer who takes your money will surely reap his just deserts one day.

我跟他在一起那麼多年了！
I have been with him for so many years!

現在妳害他，未來他也找人來對付妳，這樣冤冤相報何時了？

Now you inflict harm on him. In future, he too seeks help to get back at you. When is this vicious cycle of revenge going to end?

更何況妳執意去做的話，未來妳還會下地獄。

If you persist stubbornly, you will go to hell in future.

彼此互相傷害，這就是妳想要的愛嗎？

Both parties hurting each other, is this the kind of love you are after?

不，並不是…我不會這麼做了。

No, it's not… I will not do it anymore.

真正愛一個人，絕對不是為了要對方回頭就想盡辦法傷害他。

When you truly love a person, you will not think of all ways to inflict hurt on him, just to get him back.

做不到真心祝福對方沒關係，希望別人對妳專一的話，妳要先能夠對人專一。

It's okay if you are unable to give him your blessings. When you wish for your partner to be faithful, you must first do your part to be a loyal partner.

所以，妳要把妳的故事告訴別人，提醒大家千萬不要走妳的路。

Hence, you must share your story and warn others against going down your path.

這是一個「大善」！

This is a great virtuous act!

好。

Okay.

有首詩：
爲思佳偶情如火，
索盡枯腸夜不眠；
自古姻緣皆分定，
紅絲豈是他人牽。

A poem goes:

The heart is ablaze as you pine for your perfect mate

The endless thinking causes sleepless nights

All matches are predestined since the beginning of time.

Since when is the red thread ever strung by Man.

純真的愛 Pure Love 完

有些人命中本來就有那個運，
是他們前世行善的福報。

Some people have such luck in their
destinies because of the fortune they
accumulated through doing virtuous
deeds in their past lives.

福報？
Fortune?

是的，只要師父輕輕點撥
他們，就能獲得那筆財，

That's right. All it takes is for
an accomplished master to
gently point the way, and
they will realize that fortune.

他們要推也推不掉的。
They can't push it away
even if they do not want it.

哇—
我好羨慕…
Wow!
I'm so envious…

而吾所做的，是先以欲勾之，
再入佛智，引他們走上聖道。

What I'm doing is: use their desire
for wealth as a bait, to guide them
through the door of the Dharma,
and subsequently onto the path of
Buddhahood.

吾還會提醒，要把至少10%
的獎金捐給慈善機構。

I always remind them to donate at
least 10% of the winnings to
charity organizations.

身邊的人最清楚自己是怎樣的個性了！

The people around us will know our character best!

吾再提點你，不要把自己的福，在短短的時間內享用完喔！

Let me remind you, do not exhaust all your fortune in a short period of time!

是…

Yes…

吾看過很多人的命，

I have seen the destinies of many people.

不要以為小時候父母一直給錢是好的。

Don't assume that it is a good thing when your parents keep giving you money since young.

長大後可是很辛苦，因為自己沒有自力更生的能力，

For you may grow up and suffer, as you lack the ability to stand on your own feet,

然後就到處佔人便宜。

and leech on the fortune of other people wherever you go.

前些日子，有位年輕人
與吾共乘的士。
Some time ago, I shared a
taxi with a young man.

年輕人，你的車資沒給
我。
Young man, you have yet
to pay your taxi fare.

RUN.
跑。

下車後，他未主動還吾他
那一份車資，就回家了。
After getting off the taxi, he
did not initiate to pay for his
share of the fare and went
home.

吾没說要請他呀！
I did not say I would
pay for him!

那年輕人用了未來錢，
That young man has used
his future wealth,

用了很多人家的福，又不懂
得及時補福。
and the fortune of other people,
with no knowledge on how to
replenish his fortune in time.

要知道，人不能夠
去佔別人的便宜。
We must know not to
take advantage of
others.

還一直叫人請自己，
更為自己免費做事。
Nor should we ask others
for treats, or work for us
for free.

人，為什麼會命不好？
Why does a person have a wretched destiny?

因為一直都在佔別人的便宜。
Because he is always taking advantage of other people.

不要這樣！
Don't do this!

無底洞
Bottomless pit

因為自己在享別人的福，
Because when you enjoy the fortune of other people,

而自己的福就會一直被扣掉，一直都在賒帳。
Your own fortune is constantly shaved off, chalking up debts of fortune from the people you fleeced.

本來下一世可以轉貧為富，

You are to be a wealthy person in your next life.

但反而卻淪落到要去向別人乞討。

But alas, you fall into poverty and end up as a beggar instead.

不要佔別人的便宜。
Do not take advantage of others.

自己佔到了，自己的名聲也會臭。
Your reputation will stink even if you manage to do that.

嗯！
Yes!

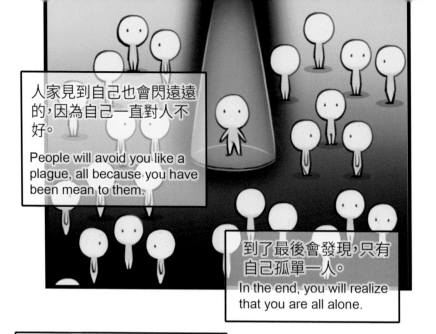

人家見到自己也會閃遠遠的，因為自己一直對人不好。

People will avoid you like a plague, all because you have been mean to them.

到了最後會發現，只有自己孤單一人。

In the end, you will realize that you are all alone.

要記得，地方的骯髒，不是來之於外表的骯髒，

Remember this, the filth of a place does not come from the physical environment,

而是人心的骯髒。

But from the muck in the hearts of the people there.

自己有錢自己買，也要願意施捨給他人，這樣才是不折不扣的大福之人。

Buy your own stuff with your own money. At the same time, have the heart to give to others. This is what truly defines a man of great fortune.

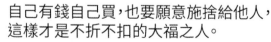

為何命不好？ Why the Wretched Destiny? 完

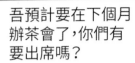

吾預計要在下個月辦茶會了，你們有要出席嗎？
I plan to conduct a Tea Session next month. Will you be attending?

不了…
No…

對呀，師父。
That's right, Master.

其實我們不想參加了，鄰居都在罵我們迷信…
We actually don't wish to participate. Our neighbours are accusing us of being superstitious…

這樣好丟臉喔！
This is so embarrassing!

沒關係，
It's okay.

你們之後要是想參加的話，吾歡迎你們。
If you wish to participate in the future, I will still welcome you.

謝謝師父。
Thank you, Master.

大家可曾想過，地球到底是個什麼樣的地方？

Have you ever wondered what kind of planet Earth are we living in?

而這地方似乎愈來愈不「妥當」，有核子危機，
And it seems that this place is getting more and more unstable. We are witnessing nuclear crisis,

有層出不窮的恐怖份子，無法預料的天災地禍，變種的新病菌……
increased terrorism threats, unpredictable natural disasters and tragedies, new mutant viruses...

讓吾告訴各位，
Let me tell you this.

這地球其實就是一所很大
的牢獄，
This planet is actually a humongous
prison,

天災地禍等即是吾等人類
的共業也。
and all the natural disasters
and tragedies are the universal
karmic retributions of us mankind.

想要不陷身其中，必需先要有出離心，然後再禮拜真正
的明師，或大善知識，
If you do not wish to be caught in it, you must first set an intention
of renunciation. Thereafter, you take refuge in a genuine and
accomplished master, or learn from a virtuous teacher,

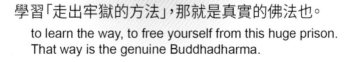

學習「走出牢獄的方法」，那就是真實的佛法也。
to learn the way, to free yourself from this huge prison.
That way is the genuine Buddhadharma.

法會、餐會或茶會的主旨，
都是在利益大家及冥陽兩利。

The main idea of the puja sessions,
tea sessions and dinner sessions
are to benefit everybody, as well as
sentient beings in the Yin and Yang
realms of existence.

茶會
Tea Sessions

餐會　Dinner Sessions

法會　Puja Sessions

坦白說，大家來或不來，對吾來說，一丁點的影響都毫無
的。

Frankly speaking, your decision to attend or miss these sessions
has absolutely no impact on me.

吾只是嘆息著，你們無福無慧，錯失如此大好機緣脫離
苦海，解掉你們身上「多條繩子」罷了。

I can only heave and sigh that you are not blessed with enough
wisdom and fortune, and hence, miss the golden opportunity to
escape from the ocean of sufferings and snip away the big mesh
of ropes that are bounding you now.

吾，玳瑚師父，絕對無自殘的傾向。

Master Dai Hu definitely has no inclination for self harm.

舉辦過年餐會、小型法會及偶爾的茶會，皆為了堅守吾在佛菩薩面前，一而再再而三所發的大願：
願將吾所學之佛法與玄學，同步利益諸有情。

Organizing these CNY dinner sessions, small-scale pujas, and the occassional tea sessions is to fulfit the great aspirations I made repeatedly in front of the Buddhas and the Bodhisattvas: I vow to use my knowledge of the Dharma and Chinese Metaphysics, to benefit all sentient beings at the same time.

有時候，吾的身體已是相當不適了，吾還是咬緊牙根地做完吾之任務，讓來者歡喜及法喜地離去。
發了願就必須去實踐之，是修行、是專一，這樣未來道果圓滿，大踏步地走出這悲情的牢獄啊！

At times, my physical body is really unwell, but I still press on to complete my mission, that is to infuse happiness and Dharma joy to those who come to me. A vow made must be actualised. That shows a singular focus towards spiritual cultivation, which shall yield the fruits of spiritual accomplishment, and the way out from this prison of gloom!

吾是修行人，本就應該任運與自在。你們來或不來，吾依然歡歡喜喜，自自在在地演化妙法音，有緣則來，無緣則去，來去皆緣也。哈......！

I am a spiritual cultivator, and lead my life in a carefree way. Whether you come for my session or not, I expound the wondrous and euphonious Dharma, with a heart of joy and ease. Those who have affinity with me will come while those without shall take their leave. It is all about affinity. Ha…!

吾等皆在這大牢獄之中，謂之為同一條船上的人，理應守望相助、向善向上、共赴蓮邦，永享極樂。要不然，就是永享極苦哦！

All of us are trapped in this huge prison. We are in the same boat, and should look out for one another, helping one another onto the path of kindness and betterment. Together, we can ascend to the Pureland and enjoy eternal bliss. If not, it will be suffering in unison!

無論法會、餐會或茶會，皆有助你們開啟那「塵封已久」的智慧，
釋放你們的靈魂，使之得大自在，永永遠遠不必再到這地球，勞改
與勞役。

Be it a puja, dinner session or a tea session, they are meant to
awake your dust-settled wisdom, and set free your spirit, never to
return to this planet Earth for corrective labour.

這樣才是真正對得起自己，也對自己的生命有所交代，善待自己
而不是刻薄自己啊！讓我們齊發力量，扭轉乾坤，大家一同改變
我們的命運吧！

Only then will you truly be able to justify to yourself and the gift
of life bestowed to you. Treat yourself with kindness, not meanness.
Let us join our hands together and turn the tide. Let us all transform
our destinies for the better!

齊發力量扭轉乾坤 Together, We Can Turn The Tide 完

自信與傲慢 Self Confidence & Arrogance

如果你的內在有一定的把握，
那個是自信，就是胸有成竹。
Self-confidence is feeling assured
internally of your own abilities.

那麼傲慢則是一個人站在孤峰上，
只看到高處的景色，
On the other hand, arrogance is like a
person standing on a mountain peak,
looking out afar at the view.

卻懶得把頭低下來，看一看
下面的景色。
But he does not care and is too
proud to look at the view beneath
him.

這就是傲慢。
That is haughtiness.

傲慢是魔的特性，因為他認為
自己是最厲害的。
Arrogance is a trait of the Mara because
an arrogant person thinks he is the best.

他的建議很爛！
His suggestion sucks!

我好厲害！
I'm so powerful!

我好強！
I'm so strong!

拒絕他！
Turn him down!

不要聽！
Don't listen!

他沒有虛心接受，
說聽聽看無妨，
He has no humility to accept
or even listen to these advice,

做為參考來提升自己目前的境界，
然後再回饋給眾生。
as a reference to elevate his own abilities
and contribute back to sentient beings.

然而，自信不是全部。
However, being self confident is not all.

最高境界的自信，是他會去幫助
別人，而不是收起來自己欣賞。
The highest form of self confidence
comes when he uses his abilities,
not for own gain and self indulgence,
but to help others.

所以，自信千萬不要變成「孤芳自賞」。
Therefore, be mindful of being overly self
confident to the extent of becoming
narcissistic.

這才是真正懂得處理自信與傲慢
之間的人。
This is the true hallmark of someone who
truly knows how to tread the fine line
between self confidence and arrogance.

自信與傲慢 Self Confidence & Arrogance 完

師父，您看。
Master, take a look.

蝸牛 Snails

有一隻非洲大蝸牛。
There's a huge African snail.

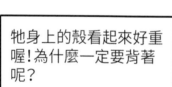

牠身上的殼看起來好重喔！為什麼一定要背著呢？

The shell on its body looks very heavy! Why must it carry it?

牠們為人時，不懂得放下種種的包袱。

When they were humans, they did not know how to put down all the life baggages.

那個殼就是牠們一直背負著過去，不願放下的因果。

The shell is a karmic manifestation of their attachments to the past, and the unwillingness to let go.

因此要一直背著一個殼，很緩慢地行走。

Thus they have a shell on its back to contend with, as they inch forward so painstakingly slow.

牠們一直吸著地，也是一種執著相。

They always stick themselves to the ground, and this is another sign of their attachment.

蝸牛就是沒有智慧，所以一直在這個慘境。

The snail possesses little wisdom, thus it is continuously in this sorrowful predicament.

我們人要向佛，學佛開啟智慧，才能夠永斷煩惱。

We humans must learn the teachings of the Buddha to ignite our wisdom, so as to put a permanent end to the endless afflictions.

那要怎麼做呢？

What should we do?

> 你要懂得放下，你不懂得放下，
> You must learn to let go. If you do not know how to let go,

> 你就會被苦苦地吸著。
> You will be miserably sucked onto.

> 我們最重要做的事，就是要求智慧。
> Our utmost important goal in life is to seek wisdom.

吾先比牠們得到智慧，因此昨晚深夜路過，看到牠們，吾就彎下腰，將吾所得到的智慧，祝福於牠們，早日脫「殼」而出。

I have gained wisdom before the snails, thus when I saw them late yesterday night, I bent down to give them my blessings, sincerely hoping that they could break free from their shells very soon.

請大家多唸7、21、49或108遍：
往生淨土，超生出苦，
南無阿彌陀佛，南無阿彌陀佛，
南無阿彌陀佛。

Please recite frequently 7, 21, 49 or 108 times:
May you ascend to the Pure Land,
And be free from the cycles of birth and all sufferings,
Namo Amituofo,
Namo Amituofo,
Namo Amituofo.

蝸牛 Snails 完

聖誕節 Christmas Day

聖誕節那天我們約哪家餐館吃飯？
Which restaurant are we dating at on Christmas Day?

那天我沒空，我要當義工。
I'm not free that day. I'm doing volunteer work.

什麼嘛！做義工有我這男朋友重要嗎？
What! Is being a volunteer more important than me, your boyfriend?

不要這樣比較啦！
Don't compare this way!

我跟大家說好要去的....
I've given my word to them that I will be going.

我不管！妳要陪我！
I don't care! You must accompany me!

可是...
But…

不可以如此強迫她聽你的話！
You cannot force her like this to listen to you!

師父...
Master...

聖誕節做什麼義工嘛！
There's no need to be a volunteer on Christmas Day!

聖誕節，是讓我們知道是聖人耶穌基督誕生，
Christmas Day is the day a Saint, Lord Jesus Christ, announced His birth to the world,

再來造福人類，傳福音的一個日子。
and was returning to benefit mankind, and spread the gospel.

所以在這神聖的一天，我們應該要去仿效聖人的理念，幫助有需要的人，
Thus, on this holy day, we ought to emulate the Saint, help the needy ones,

把愛和光明傳出去，多散發聖人所教導的禮義廉恥。
Spread love and light, and propagate the Saints' teachings of propriety, justice, integrity and honour.

比如，像她一樣去做義工，

For example, do volunteer work like her.

又或者煮早餐給父母吃，聆聽他們的心聲，給予他們慰問，

Or prepare breakfast for your parents, listen to their woes and shower them with your care and concern,

從中把快樂關愛帶給人，自己也快樂。

And in the process, bring happiness and love to others and yourself too.

愚昧地去尋歡作樂、聚會，
錢財只會花光光，連福份也倒掉，
Indulging in mindless, self-indulging
merry-making and gatherings will
only deplete your money and fortune.

身心又疲勞，到頭來問題多
又多。
You will exhaust yourself physically
and mentally, inviting more troubles
to come in the end.

最起碼，我們在聖誕節那天應該像
聖人一樣地嚴謹守著我們的戒律，
勿忘最初的發心。
At the very least, on Christmas Day,
we should strictly observe the precepts
like a Saint would, and never forgetting
our initial intention of purity.

聖誕節 Christmas Day 完

斷煩惱 Breaking Down Afflictions

怎麼了？
What's wrong?

嘆了那麼長的氣？
Why the long sigh?

唉——
Sigh…

師父...
Master…

還好吧？
Are you alright?

我在想下個月的房租，
I'm thinking about my home rental for next month,

還有昨天我和鄰居為澆花這種小事起了爭執...
And the quarrel I had with my neighbour yesterday over the petty matter of watering the plants.

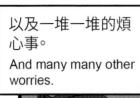

以及一堆一堆的煩心事。
And many many other worries.

想著想著就覺得一直嘆氣...
As I think, I can't help but keep sighing…

師父，為什麼人會有一堆煩惱呢？
Master, why do Man have all kinds of afflictions?

因為不知足，才會有煩惱。
Because of discontentment, hence there are afflictions.

幸福和自由你都要，那你怎麼不解開你身上的繩子呢？
You desire both happiness and freedom. Why do you not untie the many strings on your body?

祇要是在娑婆世間，煩惱就是四周圍，
As long as you are in this Saha world, you cannot escape troubles and worries.

什麼時候，什麼空間都有的。
They are all around us at any moment and space in time

這樣煩惱要怎麼消除啊？
Then how can I get rid of afflictions?

無論你怎麼想要解決煩惱都好，
No matter how much you wish to find a solution to your troubles,

如果那個時候的機緣不成熟，那件事情始終沒有解決的方法。
It is futile if the timing and affinity is not ripe.

煩惱依然還是煩惱，不如讓它就這樣去。
Your vexations remain as they are. In this case, you might as well leave your troubles alone.

你會發現，當你專注在當下所做的事情時，
煩惱反而迎刃而解了。

You will discover that when you are fully focused
in what you are doing in the present moment,
a solution to your afflictions will unexpectedly
appear.

這是吾的經驗和心得，
傳授給你。

This is my personal experience
and insights and I'm imparting
them to you.

謝謝師父！
Thank you, Master!

斷煩惱 Breaking Down Afflictions 完

心靈的餐宴 A Feast For The Soul

一個健康的體魄，對於修行而言，是非常重要的。
就算各位無福修行，擁有健康的體魄，同樣是重要
及需要的。

A healthy physical body is crucial to your spiritual practice.
It is equally important and necessary, even if you have no
fortune to engage in spiritual cultivation.

想要持有健康的體魄，秘訣就在身、口、意清淨，
以及少少心懷。而這兩部可以說，就是內外雙修也。
當中的智慧與技法，實需認禮明師不可。

The keys to a healthy body lie in the purity of your speech,
action and thoughts, as well as having a minimalist mindset.
The sum of these two factors equates to internal and external
cultivation. The succinct wisdom and nuances involved can
only be imparted by an accomplished master.

明師所以是明師，乃是因為他是明明白白，實修實證的老行家，絕對能夠引領我們一條明路，避免「暗路遭殃」啊！

An accomplished master is such, because he had walked the path before us and fully capable to guide us down the path of Light, avoiding all ambushes and obstacles!

未學佛前，吾以為躺在醫院裡的，躺在家中的，
又或者身體有狀況的，才叫病人，而自己並不在
以上的例子中，自己就不是病人。

Before I learnt the Dharma, my definition of a sick person is
one who is lying in the hospital or ailing in bed at home.
I would not consider myself a sick person if I don't fall into
the above definitions.

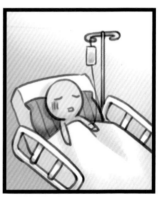

原來這種以為，是不正確的。
I realized later that I was wrong.

吾在未深入學佛前，也以為走路靠輪椅，靠拐杖，
瞎子、啞巴、耳聾......的，才是叫殘障人士。

Before I delved deep into Buddhist teachings, my definition of
disability only included people in wheelchairs, with clutches,
people who are blind, deaf or mute, etc.

各位若真是學佛的三寶弟子，就應當知曉，佛法本來就是來
對治，吾等眾生的八萬四千種病及煩惱啊！

If you are a true disciple of the Three Jewels who learns the Dharma,
you should know that the Buddha's teachings is the cure for the 84,000
ailments of the sentient beings like us!

佛說萬法唯心，這其實就是
最重要的口訣，

The Buddha says that all phenomena
arise from your mind alone.
This phrase is actually the most
critical secret formula.

吾等眾生祇要好好的，跟著佛大慈大悲的口訣，
每日不斷的實修，必能永斷煩惱，得究竟之大樂。

As long as we sentient beings adhere to this
compassionate secret formula given by the Buddha
and practice diligently everyday, we are bound to
break free from all afflictions and attain great eternal bliss.

身體有病，可向世間醫生求治。但心靈的病，就必需得向佛陀求「心樂」啊！

You can seek medical help from a doctor if you are physically ill. However, if your mind falls sick, you need to seek heart medicine from the Buddha!

試想想，誰人無貪、愛、無明、怨、憎、癡、妒等等。
眾生若無此心靈之病，佛陀也無須傳下八萬四千法，
助吾等眾生等治八萬四千種病呀！

Think about it, who is free from greed, love, ignorance, resentment, hatred, jealousy, etc? If sentient beings do not have such heart issues, Lord Buddha would not have to impart 84,000 Dharma practices,to heal us sentient beings suffering from these 84,000 afflictions!

雖說天下無不散之宴席，但所有席宴的主旨，皆為了誠意款待來賓啊！

Although all good feasts must come to an end, the main idea of a feast is to host all guests with full sincerity and hospitality!

因此，吾非常樂意地在「百忙」中，挪出那麼「非常」的時間，辦餐會與茶會等，傳授你們調適心靈的方法，使之達至安適、平穩，及柔悅的頻率。你們知道嗎？

Therefore, I gladly take time out from my busy schedule, to conduct Dinner and Tea Sessions to impart the ways of calming your own inner state, to align yourselves to the frequency of complete ease, stability and gentle joy. Do you know that?

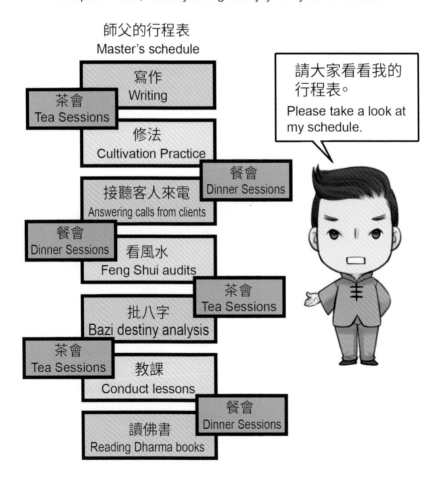

師父的行程表
Master's schedule

茶會
Tea Sessions

寫作
Writing

修法
Cultivation Practice

餐會
Dinner Sessions

接聽客人來電
Answering calls from clients

餐會
Dinner Sessions

看風水
Feng Shui audits

茶會
Tea Sessions

批八字
Bazi destiny analysis

茶會
Tea Sessions

教課
Conduct lessons

餐會
Dinner Sessions

讀佛書
Reading Dharma books

請大家看看我的行程表。

Please take a look at my schedule.

如今吾已得佛陀正法，不出來弘法利生，
怎對得起傳吾法的根本上師，大聖佛陀及
諸佛菩薩摩訶薩。
你們若是真想解脫生死苦惱，心靈的餐宴
「道道佳餚」定讓各位留連忘返，回味無
窮，歡迎入席。

Now that I am bestowed with the true Dharma from
Buddha, how can I not propagate Buddha's teachings
and bring benefits to all sentient beings? I will be
letting my Root Guru Master, the Great Sage Lord
Buddha and the rest of the Buddhas and Bodhisattvas
down, if I do not.

If you are looking for a way to liberate yourself from
the troubles and sufferings of birth and death, please
join me at the Feast for the Soul, where delectable
dishes of wisdom will be served. You will enjoy the
memorable experience so much that you entertain
no thought of leaving. Welcome to the table!

心靈的餐宴 A Feast For The Soul 完

成功的人 A Successful Person

你身邊周遭一切的人與事，都極有可能是你的助緣。

The people and matters around you are highly likely to be supportive affinities.

能不能夠把握，看你自己了。

Whether you can make good use of them, that will depend on you.

因此機會是自己給自己的，不是求別人送給你的。

Hence opportunities are to be given to you by yourself, and not begged from others to give it to you.

常常埋怨的人，非上等命的一種象徵。

A person who complains often does not exemplify a superior destiny.

真正上等命的人，他是每天都在檢討自己哪裡做得不足，哪裡做得不夠，然後去改善，去增添他的一種圓滿。

A person with a superior destiny will always reflect daily on his own inadequacies and shortcomings, take action to improve and strive towards perfection.

這，就是上等命的一個源頭。

This trait is the origin of a superior destiny.

成功的人 A Successful Person 完

做壞事的人 The Man Who Does Bad Deeds

孩子，對不起...
Sorry, my child…

爸爸忍不住做了壞事。
Daddy couldn't help…
but committed a crime…

老公...
Hubby…

爸爸...
Daddy…

快走吧！
Let's go!

媽媽，為什麼爸爸會說他忍不住呢？
Mummy, why did Daddy say he couldn't help it?

明明那是壞事不是嗎？
It was obvious that it was the wrong thing to do, wasn't it?

這...
This…

孩子...
My child…

爸爸！
Daddy!

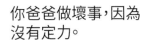

你爸爸做壞事，因為沒有定力。

Your father did the wrong thing, because he didn't have self-control.

師父...
Master...

我長大後會不會像爸爸一樣做壞事啊？

When I grow up, will I do wrong like Daddy?

只要你跟師父一樣學佛就不會想做壞事了。

As long as you learn the Dharma like Master, you will not wish to do wrong.

好，我要跟師父一樣學佛！

Okay, I will learn the Dharma like Master!

說得很好，孩子。
Well said, child.

請記住，學佛先學戒律，就是要把
自己變成一個「正當」的人。

Please remember, learning the Dharma starts
from learning the precepts, so that you can
transform yourself into a proper person.

財富來自於德，
德來自於守戒。
要擁有持續的財富，
需要守戒持戒。

All wealth stems from your virtues,
and virtues in turn come from
adhering to precepts.To have an
everlasting flow of wealth, one
needs to live by the precepts.

做壞事的人 The Man Who Does Bad Deeds 完

師父！
Master!

我跟朋友拿到您的照片喔！
I have gotten your photo from a friend!

這張！
This photo!

是什麼照片？
Which photo?

王者之風
The Air of the Victorious One

師父手上還拿著撲克牌，這樣好像賭神喔！
Master is holding poker cards in his hands, just like the God of Gamblers!

哈哈哈！ Hahaha!
你可以再看仔細一點。
Take a closer look.

咦？
Huh?

師父，我好羨慕您。
Master, I'm so envious of you.

是否我的人生要賭一把才能像您一樣呢？
Should I wager with my life to be like you?

賭的後果，總是淒慘的。
The consequences of gambling is always tragic.

人生就像一場賭局，這或許沒有太大的錯。
Life is like a gambling game of chance. Perhaps there isn't much wrong with this saying.

但這句話，不是要我們一直把生命放在賭桌上去賭，
but this doesn't mean that one should bet his life on the gambling table.

這樣，你的人生肯定完蛋。
For this will surely ruin your life.

這…
This…

王者之風 The Air of the Victorious One 完

善待自己 Treat Yourself With Benevolence

妳怎麼了？
What's wrong with you?

妳一臉難過的樣子？
Why do you look so sad?

師父，我昨晚被求婚了。
Master, I received a wedding proposal yesterday night.

但是...
But...

鈴鈴鈴鈴鈴鈴！
Ring ring ring ring ring ring!

寶貝，請嫁給我吧！
Baby, please marry me!

鈴鈴鈴鈴鈴鈴！
Ring ring ring ring ring ring！

我的豪宅、鑽石、我的心都是妳的！
My mansion, diamonds and my heart are all yours!

鈴鈴鈴鈴鈴鈴！
Ring ring ring ring ring ring!

親愛的...
Darling…

鈴鈴鈴鈴！
Ring ring ring ring!

那鈴聲一直響，我才發現原來一切都是在做夢！
The alarm kept ringing.
I then realised it was all just a dream!

沒有房子、沒有先生、沒有鑽石！
No mansion, no husband, no diamonds!

Ha ha ha!
哈哈哈！

Sob sob!
嗚哇！

那夢境真實到我以為是真的，
That dream was so realistic that I thought it was all true,

到現在心都沒有平復下來！
Until now, my heart has yet to calm down!

是的，
Yes.

人生是場大夢，
Life is like a big dream,

而睡眠中的境界，也就是人生的小夢。
Our state of sleeping is another dream state, a smaller one of Life.

道家的太極圖畫得實在好。一半白一半黑，
白中有黑點，黑中有白點。

The Taiji diagram from Taoism is a fantastic illustration.
One half of it is white, and the other black. In the white
half lies a black dot, and in the black half lies a white dot.

這當中蘊藏著修行人最終所要悟得的
真理，那就是證道。

In the diagram lies the Truth that all spiritual
practitioners must eventually comprehend,
that is, to actualize the Way.

這當中也蘊藏著罪業眾生，從這五濁惡世，
返回太虛清淨界的深密。

This Taiji diagram also holds the deep secret for all
sinned sentient beings, on how to leave this Evil World
of Five Turbidities and return to their original form in the
pristine Universe.

吾等罪業眾生，一直在六道中輪迴，

All sentient beings, including myself, have been suffering endlessly in the Six Realms of Existence through endless reincarnations.

一世一世的受盡生、老、病、死、求不得、愛憎會、五陰熾盛等眾苦，

They are being put through the sufferings of birth, old age, sickness, death, unfulfilled wishes and desires, separation from loved ones, meeting those that we dislike, the flourishing of the Five Skandhas, etc.

沒能真正享過「清福」，那是因為我們太過執著於認假為真啊！

We never really enjoy a life of peace and blessings because we are overly attached to the illusory nature of things as the reality.

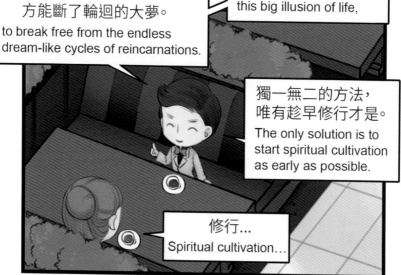

是的，且需精進不懈，
Yes, and it must be with steely determination and diligence,

願能早日修至無眼界、無意識界、無無明、亦無無明盡。
Set your intent to attain spiritual accomplishments of no sensory realm, no consciousness realm; no ignorance and also no ending of ignorance.

明白了。
I understand.

嘿！—Hey,
你看這篇報導。
Take a look at this news article!

是那個有名的出家人耶！
It's that famous monk!

報導說他沒有騙信徒，我才不相信。
The news reported that he did not deceive his devotees. I don't believe.

他搞不好都在向信徒亂說佛法，我才不相信他是真修行！
For all we know, he might be misrepresenting the Dharma to the devotees. I don't believe that he is genuinely cultivating.

因此，我們學佛修行的佛子，

Therefore, we, as students of the Dharma and spiritual cultivators,

若對於某修行人或出家僧眾有「不明白之處」，

if we have insufficient understanding of any particular monk or spiritual practitioner,

可以親近他，研究他的書、細心聆聽他的說法開示，

we can get nearer to him, study his books, and listen intently to his Dharma discourses,

可才下定論，方是學子、君子所為啊！

before we make any unbiased conclusion. This is the trait of a real learned person, a man of noble character!

千千萬萬不可人云亦云，以訛傳訛才好。

Please do not ever follow the herd and base your judgement on hearsay.

在這人世間，誹謗他人已是有罪哦！

In this mortal world, slandering is a criminal offence as well.

知道！
Got it!

妳知道嗎？
Do you know?

本是同根生，務請善待自己。

We are all born from the same source, so please treat yourself with benevolence.

善待自己 Treat Yourself With Benevolence 完

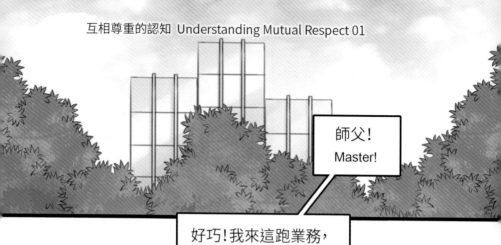

互相尊重的認知 Understanding Mutual Respect 01

師父！
Master!

好巧！我來這跑業務，
What a coincidence! I'm here to meet clients.

竟然會遇到您，師父是來看風水嗎？
Didn't expect to meet you here. Is Master here to do Feng Shui audit?

對。
好久不見了。
That's right. Been a while since we met.

71

她和她的同事們正要進去酒吧喝酒。

She and her colleagues were just about to enter the bar for drinks.

是我上司又要叫我陪他喝酒啦！

It's my manager who wants me to accompany him for drinks again!

妳不是已經皈依佛教嗎？

Haven't you taken refuge in Buddhism?

這樣不是犯酒戒嗎？

Isn't this breaking the precept of abstinence from intoxicants?

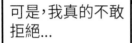

可是，我真的不敢拒絕...
But, I really dare not reject him…

....

明晚還要再去喝...
I still have to go drinking tomorrow night…

結果她騙師父您和她先生說在公司加班。
So she lied to Master and her husband that she was working overtime in the office.

竟然如此。
So this is the truth.

自己要先有守戒的精神。
You must first have the spirit to uphold the precepts

自己都不尊敬自己的信仰，自然不會有人想尊重。
If you do not respect your own faith, naturally nobody will give it the due respect too.

是的。
Indeed.

師父，快來看看，
Master, quick, take a look,

我家還有哪邊的風水要改？
Where else in my home do I need to change the Feng Shui?

這不是酒嗎？
Isn't that alcohol?

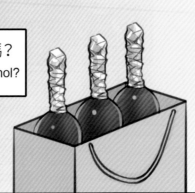

這是旅行回國時，幫老闆買的酒。
This is the liquor that I helped my boss to buy when I returned from my travels.

不是我要喝的。
It's not for my consumption.

妳與吾皈依同一位根本上師，當代法王蓮生活佛，
You and I took refuge under the same Root Guru, Dharma King Living Buddha Lian Sheng.

妳卻藐視根本上師的教義，忤逆吾的教誨。
However, you blantantly disregard His teachings and my instructions.

這也是沒辦法的事，老闆交待的嘛！
This can't be helped. It's an order from my boss!

師父，還是趕緊看看我家的風水吧！
Master, let's just quickly take a look at my home Feng Shui!

唉呀！ *Sigh!*

沒有用。
This is useless.

怎麼會？
How can that be?

妳從不好好閱讀根本上師的文集與開示，
You never diligently read the Dharma books and discourses from our Root Guru Master,

祂最近才開示：「拿酒給人喝，犯了不飲酒戒，五百世沒有手。」（如蚯蚓等動物。）
He recently expounded: If you give alcohol to others to drink, you are breaking the precept of abstinence from alcohol, and the consequence is 500 rebirths without hands.(Eg. like a millipede)

妳還想解決風水的問題，
這是治標不治本。
You still wish to resolve your
family woes with Feng Shui.
This is not solving the root
cause at all.

妳明知故犯，折了這個福，
You flout the precepts intentionally,
losing your merits,

妳認為妳未來還會有好的
發展嗎？
What good future do you think
is left for you?

其實老闆知道我在守戒，
他還勸我不必執著戒律…
My boss does know I have to
adhere by the precepts but he
advised me not to be attached
to them.

他都這麼說了，要是惹他
不開心，我怕今年的升職
就泡湯了…
Since he said so, if I still make
him unhappy, I fear that my
chances of getting a promotion
this year will be ruined…

我們所要的一切都是
建立在德。
Our merit and virtues are
the source of all that we
desire.

這樣更不對。
This is even
more wrong.

天，因爲有德，所以常覆，地有德，所以常載，

The Heaven has virtues, hence it can cover.
Earth has virtues, therefore it can sustain.

日月星有德，所以常照。
人要有德，才能夠常順、常旺、常樂。

The Sun, moon and the stars have virtues,
thus their never ending illumination;
Man must have virtues, in order to enjoy
peace, prosperity and bliss.

妳不能說妳怕拒絕，

You cannot give the
excuse that,

以免什麼會發生在妳身上。
東家不打打西家，

you fear the consequences of
saying no. There is always
another job out there.

人要有志氣，要有守戒
的精神，

A person must have higher
aspirations, and the willpower
to observe the precepts,

才會得善神的擁護。

in order to be blessed by
the virtuous gods.

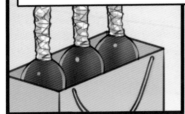

妳自己都不尊重妳的信仰，
If you do not respect your own faith,

試問人家怎麼會尊重妳的信仰呢？
how would another person respect it?

他看妳也不過是那種人，可能暗地裡還瞧不起妳，
He will not be impressed by your character, and may even secretly despise you,

這...
This…

覺得妳外表說妳已皈依，
for being a hypocrite in taking refuge,

原來妳根本沒有皈依，還是犯戒。
as you are not steadfast in upholding your precepts.

妳要走在正道上，沒有過失下，才不會損自己的福德。
You must walk on the Right Path, and not commit any sin, to ensure that your merits will not be deducted.

佛陀涅槃時，已囑咐佛弟子要
「以戒為師」。

When Lord Buddha was about to enter
Nirvana, He already exhorted that all
disciples must take the precepts as
their teacher.

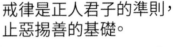

戒律是正人君子的準則，
止惡揚善的基礎。

Precepts are the cornerstone of an
upright and righteous human being,
the foundation of spreading
goodness and curbing the
non-virtuous in us.

做為一個老闆，一個上司，
必須要以德服人。

As a boss, as a superior, you must
command the respect of your
subordinates with your merits and
virtues.

下屬因為是你的員工，
她當然不敢得罪你，冒
犯你，

It is natural that your subordinate
will not dare to offend you,

因爲她需要這個薪水來養家或過活。
because she needs the salary to make a living or feed her family.

就算她爲了順從你，而犯戒，
你在她心中的形象一定大打折扣。
Even if she follows your instructions, at the expense of flouting her precepts, deep in her heart, she will think lesser of you.

如果有一天，她有了另外一份工作邀約，她一定不考慮就走，
If one day she receives another job offer, she will not hesitate to leave you,

因爲她覺得你是一個敗德的上司，不值得她忠心。
because she feels that you are lacking in virtues and unworthy of her loyalty.

如果她留下來，那必定只有一個原因，因爲她也敗德。
If she stays on, then it must be for the reason that she too is lacking in virtues.

敗德的上司 + 敗德的下屬，
能做出什麼好成績來？
A non-virtuous superior + a non-virtuous employee, what good result can they produce?

互相尊重的認知 Understanding Mutual Respect 03

醫 院
Hospital

師父，
我公公他...
Master, my
father-in-law…

對...
That's right…

醫生剛剛取出很多
膽結石，
The doctor just taken
out many gall bladder
stones,

因喝酒喝壞了
身體？
His alcoholism
damaged his health?

還割了他的膽。
and also removed his
gall bladder.

互相尊重的認知 Understanding Mutual Respect 03

雖然我們一家都是佛教徒，但是我公公就是愛喝酒。

Although our whole family are Buddhists, my father-in-law likes to drink.

還常常叫我老公買酒給他喝。

And he often asks my husband to buy him liquor.

公公再這樣下去對身體不好，還違背戒律。

If he continues this way, his health will suffer and this is breaking the precepts.

所以我有勸老公和大家都不要買酒給他，

So I did advise my husband and the family not to buy alcohol for him.

可是...
But...

你這兒子沒有用啦！
You are a useless son!

還是你弟妹最乖，會買酒孝敬我！
Your younger brother and sister are most filial. They will buy liquor for me!

爸爸...
Dad...

公公...
Father-in-law...

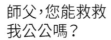

師父，您能救救
我公公嗎？

Master, can you save
my father-in-law?

我會以玄學來幫助妳
公公能早日康復。

I will use Chinese Metaphysics
to help your father-in-law to
have a speedy recovery.

謝謝您！
Thank you!

喝酒的人愚癡，送酒的人愚孝。

Deluded is the man who drinks.
Ignorant is the filial children
who feed his alcoholism.

喝酒，會亂人本性，生出無量的過失，

Drinking alcohol creates chaos to the human
nature, and countless sins arise,

如酒後駕駛、醉酒打人、儀態盡失、
胡言亂語、淫慾熾盛、惡人相近等等。

such as drunk driving, drunk fighting,
loss of etiquette, blabbering of nonsense,
sexual indecency, attracting bad company,
etc.

吾，玳瑚師父，滴酒不沾，
I, Master Dai Hu, have abstained from intoxicants for over a decade,

任何有酒精的食物，吾也不食。
不飲酒者，有何果報？
and neither do I consume food with alcohol in it. What are the merits from such abstinence?

意念清明，智慧超群，
不會精神分裂、
Beside mental clarity and supreme wisdom, one will not be stricken with schizophrenia,

不會神智恍惚、
不會胡思亂想，
更不會被迷惑。
mental disarray, mental disturbance and fall prey to temptations.

互相尊重的認知 Understanding Mutual Respect 完

知恩莫忘報 Do Not Forget The Help Received

多年渡眾，吾發現，很多能夠
找到吾的客人，

After many years of delivering
sentient beings, I have come to
realize the reason why many
clients are able to contact me.

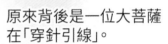

原來背後是一位大菩薩
在「穿針引線」。

A great Bodhisattva has
been playing the role of
our middleman.

祇要是菩薩安排來的，
吾都會有種「非見不可」
的感覺，

Whenever the Bodhisattva
sends a client along my way,
I will have this uncanny feeling
that I must make time to meet
this person.

而往往這些客人也很快就能見到
吾，得到吾的協助。

More often than not, such clients would
quickly be able to make an appointment
with me and get my help.

見了面後，才知道其實是菩薩給吾的工作，是吾的榮幸，
After the meeting, I will discover that it is yet another assignment bestowed upon me by the Bodhisattva. It is my honour.

更是菩薩「千處祈求千處應，苦海常作渡人舟」的宏願。
This is a manifestation of the great aspiration made by the Bodhisattva, to answer the thousand prayers from a thousand hearts, while guiding and delivering people, in the ocean of sufferings, over to the shore of enlightenment.

所以吾也常告訴這些客人，一定要懂得感恩「南無觀世音菩薩」的慈悲救渡啊！
So I often remind these clients that they must show gratitude for the compassionate salvation from Avalokiteshvara Bodhisattva!

如果沒有祂，恐怕很多眾生無法從逆境中走出來。

Without Him, many sentient beings would have never been able to walk out from their adversities.

祂對我們眾生的貢獻，實在無法用文字來比擬。

The contributions to us sentient beings from the Bodhisattva are so great that words cannot suffice.

家家彌陀佛，戶戶觀世音，

The Chinese saying goes: every family knows the name of Amitabha Buddha, every household worships the Avalokiteshvara Bodhisattva.

很多時候我們得到祂的加持與守護，可是我們卻渾然不知。
Many a time, we are unaware that we have been receiving protection and blessings from the Bodhisattva all along.

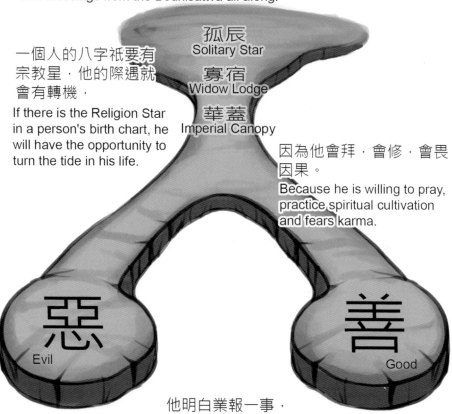

一個人的八字祇要有宗教星，他的際遇就會有轉機，
If there is the Religion Star in a person's birth chart, he will have the opportunity to turn the tide in his life.

孤辰
Solitary Star

寡宿
Widow Lodge

華蓋
Imperial Canopy

因為他會拜，會修，會畏因果。
Because he is willing to pray, practice spiritual cultivation and fears karma.

惡
Evil

善
Good

他明白業報一事，
The person understands retribution.

勤於修善斷惡，進而改寫自己的命運。
He diligently cultivates the seeds of merits and eradicates the roots of unwholesomeness, rewriting his destiny for the better.

農曆二月十九日，是「南無大慈大悲觀世音菩薩」的佛辰。

The 19th day of the 2nd Lunar month, is the holy birthday of Namo Avalokiteshvara Bodhisattva.

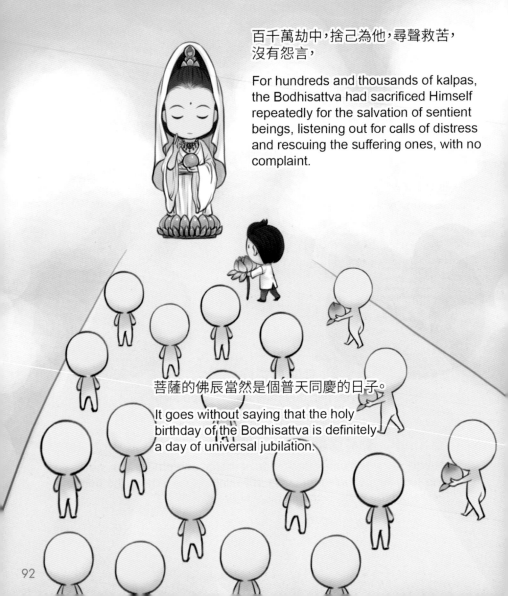

百千萬劫中，捨己為他，尋聲救苦，沒有怨言，

For hundreds and thousands of kalpas, the Bodhisattva had sacrificed Himself repeatedly for the salvation of sentient beings, listening out for calls of distress and rescuing the suffering ones, with no complaint.

菩薩的佛辰當然是個普天同慶的日子。

It goes without saying that the holy birthday of the Bodhisattva is definitely a day of universal jubilation.

楞嚴經記載，持誦「南無觀世音菩薩」的聖號，能得十四無畏：

The Śūraṅgama Sūtra states that recitation of the Holy Name of the Avalokiteshvara Bodhisattva brings forth the 14 Fearlessness Powers:

火難無畏
Fearlessness from fire calamity

苦惱無畏
Fearlessness from afflictions

風難無畏
Fearlessness from wind calamity

Namo Guan Shi Yin Pu Sa
南無觀世音菩薩

鬼難無畏
Fearlessness from evil ghosts

兵難無畏
Fearlessness from weapon attacks

盜難無畏
Fearlessness from robbery

獄難無畏
Fearlessness from imprisonment

貪欲無畏
Fearlessness from desires and cravings

瞋恚無畏
Fearlessness from anger and hatred

愚痴無畏
Fearlessness from ignorance

求男無畏
Fearlessness from wanting a son

持名無畏
Fearlessness from reciting the Holy Name

求女無畏
Fearlessness from wanting a daughter

在法華經中，釋迦牟尼佛也曾讚歎，此功德不可思議！

In the Saddharma Pundarika Sutra, Lord Shakyamuni Buddha had also sung praises of the inconceivable merits in reciting the name of Avalokiteshvara Bodhisattva.

南無觀世音菩薩的十二大願中，誓將滅除三惡道。

One of the Twelve Great Vows of Avalokiteshvara Bodhisattva is to eradicate the Three Evil Paths of Existence.

餓鬼道

Hungry Ghosts Realm

因此能得人身，能聞佛法，
皆由菩薩的恩德而來。

Hence, to be born a human who gets to hear of the Dharma is made possible by the grace and kindness of Avalokiteshvara Bodhisattva.

畜生道

Animal Realm

若輪為畜生，變成雞狗牛羊，

If we are born in the animal realm, as chickens, dogs, cows and goats,

地獄道

Hell Realm

如何能供養觀世音菩薩，
並向祂懺悔呢？

How can we repent and make offerings to Avalokiteshvara Bodhisattva?

能夠懺悔供養是自身的福德，更是消除累世業障的開始。

It is a blessing if we are able to do repentance and offering practices, as that marks the start of eradicating our karmic debts from many past lives.

普陀山上，天人常向菩薩獻供，修福報恩。

On the top of Mount Putuo, heavenly beings often descend to make their offerings to Avalokitesvara Bodhisattva, to cultivate their fortune and repay their gratitude.

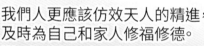

我們人更應該仿效天人的精進，及時為自己和家人修福修德。

We should emulate the diligence of the devas and quickly do the same cultivation of merits and virtues for ourselves and our families.

讀者粉絲們，千萬不要錯過這個息災敬愛增益的好日子啊！

My dear fans and readers, do not miss out on this great day to eradicate your calamities, improve your inter-personal relationships and enhance your resources!

知恩莫忘報 Do Not Forget The Help Received 完

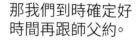

那我們到時確定好時間再跟師父約。
We will fix an appointment with Master once we confirm the date.

好，請慢走。
Sure, take care.

師父好厲害。
會好幾樣的事情。
Master is so amazing. You are capable of so many things.

因為我能一心二用。
Because I can do two things at once.

我就不行。
I can't do that.

要怎麼做才能一心二用呢？
How can I do two things at one time?

不能分心的人，就先專注自己的精力在一件事。
If you cannot multi-task, it is wise to fully focus your energy on a singular task.

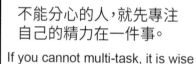

這樣，成就會比較早，
人也會比較開心，

You will achieve success much earlier, and be happier this way.

不會因為什麼都沒有，
而起煩惱心和怨心。

There will not be any resentment or worry when you feel you are under-achieving.

人會敗，有時就是敗在一個
「貪」，及「不自量力」。

One's failure is often due to greed, in wanting to do all things at the same time, without measuring your own abilities.

明白了。
謝謝師父。

I understand now.
Thank you, Master.

專注 Focus 完

爲情而生的女人 The Woman Who Lives For Love

我好害怕他會因此離開我，
I'm so afraid that he will leave me because of this,

那我之後要怎麼生活呢？
How am I going to live after this?

不要把生命只放在感情上。
感情沒有了，還有家人。

Do not commit your entire life to matters of the heart.

Without romance, there's still your family.

可是...
But...

一個人也可以生活。
感情這東西，往往是一個業障。
You can still live life to the fullest even if you are single. Romance is often a karmic obstacle in life.

一想到他說的那些話，我就難過的想死…
When I recall what he said, I'm so upset that I wish to end my life…

我想要讓他痛苦！
I wish to make him suffer!

妳自己也是一條珍貴的生命，
Your life is just as precious.

怎麼可以用這樣的理由輕易放棄！
How can you use such a reason to give up so easily?

Master...
師父...

生命如花籃，不要埋沒
自己的才華。
Life is like a basket of flowers,
so do not bury your talents.
師父/Master

不要把整個人生放在
一個人的身上。
Do not invest your lifetime
in any one person.
師父/Master

但是...
我一直覺得他是我的
好姻緣。
But...I had always felt that
he is the one who will give
me a good marriage.

如果有一天失去了他，妳也
不至於沒有了精神依靠，而
走上不歸路。
One day if he leaves you, you will
not be lost with no mental support
or motivation, ending up on the
road to suicide.

嫁個好老公，娶個好老婆，
都是我們前世修來的福報。
A fulfilling marriage is the result of
merits cultivated from our previous
lives.

現在的年代已不一樣了。
Times are very different now.

不祇是看風水不能用一樣的方法，
Not only do Feng Shui techniques have to evolve to fit modern people's needs,

女性也得從廚房走出來，
women should also step out of the kitchen,

不要把全部生命放在老公與子女身上。
and not pine her entire hope and life on her husband and children.

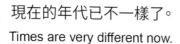

做人不要短見。
Do not be short-sighted.

人生有很多條路，不祇是好姻緣
這一條路而已，
There are many roads leading to Rome.
A good marriage is not all that matters.

況且這些都不是解脫的路子。
Furthermore, these mundane worldly paths do not lead to Liberation.

爲情而生的女人 The Woman Who Lives For Love 完

調色板 Colour Palette

師父，您的ideas好多喔！

Master, you have so many ideas!

是呀，真不知您是如何辦到的？

Exactly, I have no idea how you can do that.

能告訴我們方法嗎？

Can you tell us your method?

不知不覺的，吾已從一個「沒有idea的小伙子」，變成「充滿ideas的大傢伙」。

Unknowingly over the years, I have transformed, from a clueless young man to an accomplished master full of ideas.

這整個過程，都歷經了憧憬，徬徨、迷惘、挫折等等，

This entire journey took me through the depths of hope, anxiety, hopelessness, defeat, etc,

漸漸「穩定」下來之後，才得以成爲眾人欲尋得的「標準」善知識，

Before I finally emerged as a up-to-standard virtuous master sought after by many

專爲人排憂解難，指點迷津的「大傢伙」。

to solve their woes and sufferings and point them in the right direction. Ha ha ha!

哇，好辛苦。
Wow, that's tough.

哈哈哈！ Hahaha!

這也是一個凡夫俗子，到覺行圓滿的佛，的必經之路。

It is a necessary path taken by a mortal enroute to becoming a Buddha with perfection of the enlightened practice.

也是從苦惱，走到極樂的必經之路，實無一人可倖免。

This is also the only path that delivers you from suffering in afflictions to eternal bliss, with no exception for anybody.

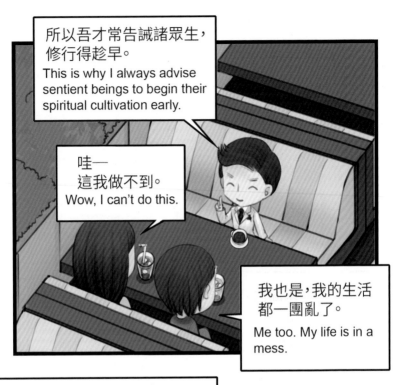

所以吾才常告誡諸眾生，修行得趁早。

This is why I always advise sentient beings to begin their spiritual cultivation early.

哇——
這我做不到。

Wow, I can't do this.

我也是，我的生活都一團亂了。

Me too. My life is in a mess.

人生不如意，是十之八九的。因我們在多世的輪迴中，有數不清的「糾結」，

Life throws at us unpleasant situations more often than not. That is because in our many past rebirths, we accumulated countless "entanglements",

而這些過去世的「糾結」，

And these past "entanglements"

是我們自做後，自受的一種循環，半點都怪不得他人。

are the "fruits" of our past actions. You cannot blame anyone else for this.

你們若明白這點，既有了「認命」的開始，

When you understand this concept, you are starting to accept your own destiny.

未來的善知識，必現於你們的生命中。

Virtuous masters will surely come into your life,

善知識傳授你們解開「糾結」的法門，還你們「本來面目」。

To impart you the wisdom to break the deadlock of these "struggles" and reveal your true nature.

我們的「本來面目」？

Our true nature?

那是什麼？

What is that?

會不會是鬼啊？

Could it be ghosts?

好恐佈...

Sounds terrifying...

當然不是。

Of course not.

「本來面目」絕對不是非人（鬼）。

Definitely not a non-human (ghost)!

而是你們清淨無染的佛性。

It is your pure and untainted Buddha nature.

佛性…
Buddha nature…

妳聽得懂師父說的嗎？

Do you understand what Master said?

若還是不明白，請繼續參研下去，記住這句話失敗乃成功之母。

If you don't, please continue to study it. Remember this, Failure is the Mother of all Success.

倘若你們自認自己為「笨笨公司」的職員，都不打緊，

If you feel that your intellect is low, do not worry.

因佛法有「八萬四千種法門」，來對治吾等眾生「八萬四千種煩惱」。

There are 84,000 different forms of Dharma practices to address the 84,000 different kinds of sufferings of us sentient beings.

對呀!
That's right!

哈哈! Haha!

師父您越說讓我們
二人越糊塗了。

Master, the more you
say, the more confused
we are.

一提到「八萬四千種法門」
與對治,

The mention of 84,000 different
Dharma practices and the issues
they address,

對一般人而言,簡直就是
丈八金剛摸不著頭腦。

Is usually incomprehensible to
the laymen.

但,若吾以我們在作畫前,準備顏料的調色板,來解釋
「八萬四千種法門」與對治,

But if I illustrate the above concept, with the colour palette an
artist uses to prepare colours before he starts a piece of art,

相信你們會較容易心領神會。

I'm sure you will find it easier to gain a
tacit understanding.

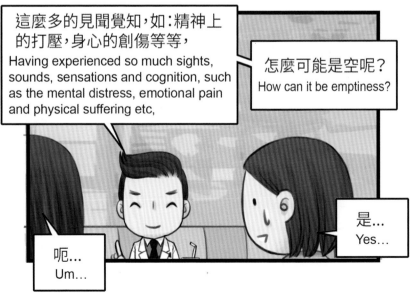

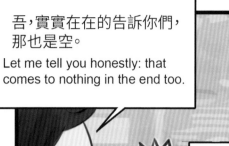

夢醒後自知，那祇是夢一場。
一場夢，始終歸爲空。
we will realise it was just a dream when we awake. A dream that culminates to nothing in the end.

Pop
碰

Pop
碰

聽過...
Heard of it before...

嗯...
Hum

到頭來什麼都沒有擁有到，
什麼都帶不走喔！
You do not own anything in the end, you can't bring anything with you!

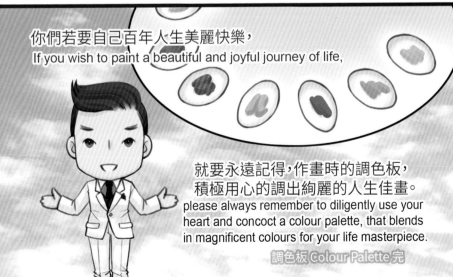

你們若要自己百年人生美麗快樂，
If you wish to paint a beautiful and joyful journey of life,

就要永遠記得，作畫時的調色板，
積極用心的調出絢麗的人生佳畫。
please always remember to diligently use your heart and concoct a colour palette, that blends in magnificent colours for your life masterpiece.

調色板 Colour Palette 完

113

最近生意好不容易有起色了，
It was really not easy for my business to pick up recently,

現在卻因為要繳稅又得花一大筆錢...
And now I have to spend a large sum of money to pay the taxes.

你怎麼能如此做呢？
How can you do that?

爲什麼我們應該認真地報稅繳稅？
Why should we take a serious view when filing income tax and paying our taxes?

這個問題你有思考過嗎？
Have you ever pondered over this issue?

這...
This…

爲什麼要報稅,爲什麼
要繳稅?

Why do we have to file and pay
our tax dues?

一、佛告訴我們要
報答四重恩。

1. The Buddha expounded
on the Four Debts of
Gratitude.

這四重恩當中一個,就是國恩。

One of them refers to the kindness of our
country that one should repay.

國恩...
Kindness of
our country?

二、沒有國,哪有家。沒有家,哪有
你我。

2. There is no home without a nation,
and when there is no home, there will
be no us.

三、老實報稅是一種誠實。

3. When we file our taxes truthfully,
we are exemplifying the trait of
honesty.

你生在這個國土，運用這國土的資源來賺取你的生計，本來就應該繳稅。

You are born in this land and have utilised its resources to make your living. It is only right to contribute taxes to the nation.

我國的稅率已是全世界當中比較低的，你還要逃。

The tax rates in this country are one of the lowest in the world, and yet you still attempt to evade taxes.

那如果把你放在那些稅率高達幾十巴仙的國家，

Imagine if you are living in other countries with higher tax rates,

看你怎麼過日子。

How are you going to survive?

這....
This…

四、這當中除了關係到誠實以外，還有關係到佛教五戒中的「偷盜」。
4. Besides honesty, it also involves the Buddhist five precepts, the precept of not stealing.

這些在在都是因因果果。
Karma is always prevalent.

我們做什麼事情，並不是吾告訴你不要告訴別人，就真的沒有人知。
No matter what we do, it is not a simple matter of me asking you to keep mum and no one will find out for real.

我們一日六時，從白天到黑夜，所做的，分秒都有神明在監察著，
Our every action and thought in every moment, from dusk till dawn, are monitored by the gods.

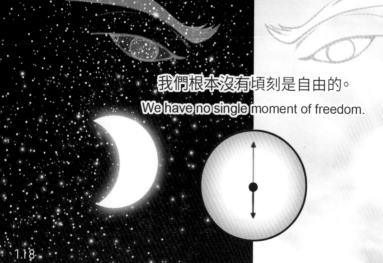

我們根本沒有頃刻是自由的。
We have no single moment of freedom.

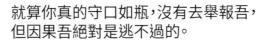

就算你真的守口如瓶，沒有去舉報吾，
但因果吾絕對是逃不過的。

Even if you kept mum and did not blow the
whistle on my misdeed, karma is already in
motion and I definitely cannot escape from its
clutches.

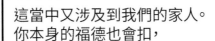

這當中又涉及到我們的家人。
你本身的福德也會扣，

Our family members will also be
implicated. Your merits will greatly
diminish,

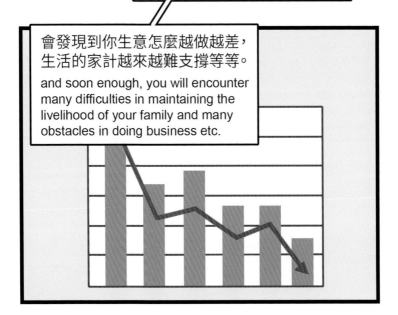

會發現到你生意怎麼越做越差，
生活的家計越來越難支撐等等。

and soon enough, you will encounter
many difficulties in maintaining the
livelihood of your family and many
obstacles in doing business etc.

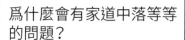

爲什麼會有家道中落等等
的問題？

Why are all these straitened
circumstances happening to
my family?

因爲你曾經蓄意逃稅，
不要繳稅。

Because you had intentionally
evaded taxes,

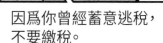

這個就是偷盜。

This is an act of stealing,

不老實，沒有報國恩，沒有
與國家一起共進退的心。

Dishonesty and failure to repay
the kindness of your country.
Neither do you have the heart to
share the weal and woe with
your motherland.

這些在在都有很多
過失。

All these make up many
misdeeds.

120

所以請你們再三地深思
吾玳瑚師父這段話。

Therefore, please think thrice about my words.

如果你們過去有逃稅的
行為,各位說沒有人告
訴過其嚴重性,

If you have committed tax evasion previously, and you protest that no one has told you of the karmic consequences,

但現在你們讀到了,請你們就馬上不要重蹈覆轍,
以免未來的未來不堪設想。

you have no excuse now after reading this article. Please do not continue with your ignorance immediately, before things go awry in the future.

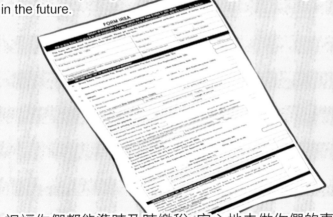

祝福你們都能準時及時繳稅,安心地去做你們的事業,
不用提心吊膽,一切皆圓滿。

Wishing everyone a happy time reporting your tax timely and accurately. Go forth in peace to excel in your career, with no fear, and all will be well.

心安理得做事業 Do Your Business With A Peace of Mind 完

沒有命運的人 The Man With No Destiny

貴為師父近二十年，真實知曉普天下，
In my past 20 years as a Master, I truly know

想要預知自己窮通禍福的人，始終多過
於不想預知自己窮通禍福的人。
that the vast majority of people do wish to
know the fortunes of their entire lives.

那為何會如此？
其實啊！這當中也是因果兩個字。
Why is that so? Well, it has all to do with Cause & Effect.

就好比一個人的信仰，「表面」看似非常虔誠，
For example, a person may appear to be very pious towards his religion,

前世
Past life

今世
Present life

事實上是多世，或前世的因，而結成今世的果，
就是這樣而已。
but in truth, it is an affinity from his many past lives, or his
previous life, that bear fruit this life.

但當中也有變數的，所以才會有「變卦」這兩個字。
而「變卦」這兩個字，其實是出自於《易經》也。
But, there always exists a possibility of change, and this
phenomena comes from I Ching, the Book of Changes.

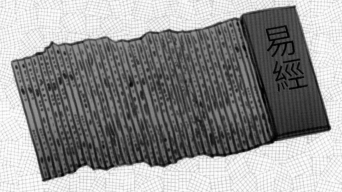

高明的玄學師父，真的一眼就能「看穿」我們的。
An brilliant Metaphysics Master can easily see through us.

那這高明的師父，是憑什麼來「看穿」我們的
「狀況」的呢？
How can he see through our situation？

「上帝」造人類時，早已將命運軌跡的密碼，分佈
在我們的骨骼、五官、掌紋及生辰四柱中。
When God created Man, He left traces of Man's destiny in
his body: our bones, facial features, palm lines and four
pillars of our birth charts.

因此,高明的師父,就是從這些命運軌跡的密碼,給我們
指點迷津的。
Therefore, a brilliant Master is able to decipher these destiny codes
and point us to the right direction.

想學得這上等的學問,並非易事。
It is not an easy task to master this body of
high wisdom.

除了要看根器與天賦,後天的努力與德行,
也是非常重要的。
Apart from one's capacity and innate gift, hard work and
virtues are very important too.

一個無福碰於高明之士的人，其一生自然而然的，
就得走在其命運的軌道上，無法自主。

When a person does not have sufficient fortune to meet an
accomplished Master, his life will naturally be dictated by his
destiny, not by his self will.

那是因為一般的人並無
修行，
That is because the typical
person does not cultivate
himself spiritually,

每一世皆是上一世及累世
的福德善惡因果演化。
and every reincarnation is the
fruition of the virtuous and
non-virtuous causes
from his accumulated
lifetimes and previous
life.

喜 Happiness

怒 Anger

哀 Sorrow

樂 Joy

受盡生時的喜、怒、哀、
樂，受盡死後的輪迴之苦。
He will experience happiness, rage,
sadness and joy while living, and the
pains of reincarnation after death.

輪迴 Reincarnation

輪迴這兩個字，真是用得佳妙。
還在輪迴中的各位，當然也就還有命運。
The word Reincarnation is so cleverly used. You, who are
still reincarnating, will of course have a destiny.

還有命運的人，很難完全的自在，
更不用談什麼自主與任運啊！
It is very difficult for a person with a
destiny to be at ease. Let's not even
talk about free will and freedom!

還有命運的人，一定是
「祂主」的。
A person who is chained to his
destiny is dictated by Destiny.

有「祂主」是不會有真正自由的一天的。
懂嗎？明白嗎？
A person controlled by Destiny will never have a day of true
freedom. Do you understand?

吾，玳瑚師父，非常讚嘆沒有
命運的人，也嚮往之。
I am full of praise for people with no
destiny and aspire to such
accomplishment.

天天老老實實地實修佛法，
已漸漸地脫離命運的軌道，
Through daily diligent honest
practice of the Dharma, I am
gradually derailing from the
tracks of Destiny.

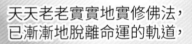

相信不久的未來，吾就能返回虛空界。
I believe I'll be able to return to Emptiness very soon in the future.

但事實上，你們只要修行得證了，你們就是一個沒有命運的人了，返不返回虛空界，都是一樣快樂得不得了。

In truth, once you attain Perfection in your spiritual cultivation, you are a person with no Destiny. Whether you return to the Void or not, you will be in a state of bliss.

有命運就有生死，有生死就有壽命的約束，依然逃脫不了苦、苦、苦。

Destiny brings about birth and death, which sets limitations on life span. There is still no escape from sufferings and more sufferings.

苦 Sufferings

苦 Sufferings

苦 Sufferings

苦 Sufferings

若你妳自認有智慧，有與無命運的人，你們會選擇做哪一個？

If you think you have the wisdom, who would you choose to be: the man with destiny, or the one without?

沒有命運的人 The Man With No Destiny 完

127

你的命你的運 Your Destiny & Fortune

普天之下，想要知曉自己命運的人，
為數之多，有如天上繁星啊！

The number of people in this world who
wish to know their destiny is as numerous
as the stars in the sky!

師父，想要知曉自己的命運
有錯嗎？是迷信嗎？

Master, is it wrong to want to know
our destiny? Is it superstitious?

都沒有錯，也非迷信。

It is neither wrong nor
superstitious.

若要論迷信，應屬那類認為
批命，可以解決一切問題的
人，

If you want to talk about superstition,
I would regard people who think by
knowing their destiny all their
problems can be solved,

以及認為命是無法
改的人。

and people who think
destiny can't be changed.

迷者不悟也。欲想知曉自己命運者，
應持有勵志改命的心，此為非迷信者。

A superstitious person has no understanding. If
you wish to know your destiny, you should have
the determination to change your fate so that
you will not be superstitious.

而這類的人，也必能改善
自己的命運。

People of such perseverance
will be able to better their lives.

師父，為什麼您認為批命能
解決一切問題的人，是屬迷
信之類呢？

Master, why do you regard people,
who think by knowing their destiny
and all problems will be solved, as
superstitious?

大多的人，只想聽到好的
一面。

Most people only wish to hear the
favourable things about their life,

不坦然也不積極的
面對，

and turn a deaf ear to
the rest,

所以也就沒興趣、沒耐性的聽與請教為他們
批命的師父，開示改命及立命之法。

Hence they don't have the interest and patience, to
listen and ask for the Master's advice on how to
alter their destiny and establish their own.

因此，吾才說這類的人，
始終歸類於迷信者也。

This is why I said such people
are considered superstitious.

師父，那他們到底迷信
些什麼？

Master, what are they
superstitious about?

他們不是迷信些什麼，他們是
迷信於他們，那不切實際的信
念，

It isn't about a particular thing.
They are just obsessed with their
impractical beliefs.

以為那些命中不好的部份，
不去聽，不去想就沒事。

They think by not listening and
thinking about the imperfections
in their destiny, all will be fine

這就吾所謂的，不坦然、
不積極也。

Thus, I say they are being
dishonest and lazy.

對於這樣的眾生，吾還是
尊重他們的決定的，
To this group of sentient beings,
I still respect their decision,

同時也給予他們加持
與祝福，福慧增長。
and give my empowerment &
blessings to the growth of their
wisdom and merits.

吾，玳瑚師父，選擇聽後再向那位，為吾批命的
師父，討教改善吾命運的方法。
I will choose to hear the Master who decodes
my destiny, and seek his advice to better my
own lot.

因為，吾可不想走啊走的，忽然一聲撲通，
掉進坑洞中，那就真的是，阿彌陀佛嘍！
As I do not wish to drop into a pothole, with an
unexpected loud thud, as I walk along in my life
journey. That would be really "Amitabha"!

其實啊!
Actually,

若你是一個,強行自己主張的人,
本就不應去找師父,為你批命呀!
if you tend to insist on your own views,
you are better off not seeking a Master
to analyse your destiny!

一個強行自己主張的人,是不會
一百巴仙,遵照師父所給予的改
命與立命之法。
A person who thinks that he is always
right will not follow the Master's advice
to a T, to improve and formulate his
own destiny

師父,我很好奇,您到底
準到什麼程度呢?
Master, I'm curious. Just how
accurate are you?

吾只需一眼望向你,
就知你是否在運中。
A look at you is all I need
to tell if you are in luck.

亦可從你的髮質,吐氣、身色(皮膚
之光澤)、眼神,等等,知曉你「近
況如何」。

I can also read your current fortunes from
your hair texture, your breath, your skin
tone and radiance, your eyes, etc.

更神的是，你走過吾身邊，吾即可知你，旺與行運否。

The most amazing thing is you just have to walk past me, and I can know if you are in luck or not.

這也是客人對吾，「又愛又恨」的原因啊！

This is why some clients have a "love-hate" relationship with me!

觀讀此漫畫後，你若還搞不清楚，應找何人規劃你一生的命運的話，

Ha! After reading this article, if you are still unsure who to engage to plan your destiny,

那真的就是你的造化了。也是你的命，你的運啊！

then it is really your own doing, your destiny, your fortune!

你的命你的運 Your Destiny & Fortune 完

改不了命的人 The Man Who Can't Change His Destiny

師父，救救我吧！
我怎麼這樣倒楣啊！
Save me, Master!
How can I be so
unlucky?

怎麼了？
What
happened?

工作那麼多年還是助理，
升遷機會都輪不到我。
I'm still a assistant after
working so many years.
Promotions always pass
me by.

交往多年的女友還劈腿！
我的錢全都花在她身上耶！
My girlfriend of many years
cheated on me!
All my money was spent
on her!

師父您能幫我改變
命運嗎？
Master, can you
help me change
my destiny?

不行。
No.

為什麼？
Why?

人的命運之所以不能改，因為他
的心無法心平氣和。
Some people are unable to
turn their Destiny around,
because of their inability to
maintain a harmonious state
of mind and Qi.

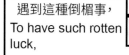

遇到這種倒楣事，
To have such rotten luck,

我怎麼可能還心平氣和呢？
how can I still stay calm?

心浮氣躁，命運祇會越來越坎坷。
When you are vexed, your life will only get rougher.

所以想要改命，先要學會心平氣和。
So to change your destiny, first learn how to keep your mind and Qi in harmony.

幸福，是自己修來的。
Happiness comes from your own cultivation.

苦命，同樣也是自己修來的。
A wretched fate is also of your own doing.

改不了命的人 The Man Who Can't Change His Destiny 完

135

城隍廟

那是城隍廟。
That is the City God Temple.

師父,我初次來這裡,那間是什麼廟呢?
Master, it's my first time here. What temple is that?

不由人算 Not up to man

有很多城隍廟裡會看到上方掛著一個碩大的算盤喔!
In many City God temples, you will see a huge abacus displayed high on a wall.

算盤?
好特別呀!
Abacus?
How special!

算盤上方的匾,還會提這四個字「不由人算」。
Inscribed on a plaque above the abacus are 4 Chinese characters, translated as "It is not in Man's hands"

136

這四個字的真實義是：我們人，依然屬於低級的靈，因爲功德不高尚也，而且人還是存著陰跟陽，也就是光明的一面和黑暗的一面。

The true meaning of these 4 characters is: We humans still belong to the lower spiritual beings, because of ignoble merits and virtues. Also, Yin and Yang remain present in Man i.e. He has his righteous side, as well as a dark side.

但吾認爲，一般人，黑暗的一面
是多過光明的一面。

But in my opinion, the dark side of
a typical man is more prevalent.

「不由人算」，是指你所做的一切，
你不能爲自己辯解，

"It's not in your hands" means
in whatever you do, you cannot
defend for yourself

說你認爲以你的邏輯，你有限的思維
空間，而認爲你所做的事情，是正當
的。

that based on your logic and
limited thinking, you think what you
do is just.

可是...那該由誰來
判斷呢？

But...who should
be the judge?

城隍廟

這些都必須由正神,來真正的判斷你的行爲,是否正確,而不是由你。
Judgement of your behaviour must be meted out by a virtuous God, not the mortal in you.

因爲你始終是在業障當中,是不清靜的,是混沌的,
As you are mired in karmic obstacles, you are impure and chaotic

所以必須由清明的正神,來執司你的善跟惡果。
Thus, it requires a clear-minded virtuous God to adjudicate your virtuous and evil karma.

所以「千算萬算不由人算」,無論你如何精打細算企圖掩飾自己的過錯,
As such, it is pointless to crack your brain for ways to conceal your own misdeeds.

你終究難逃城隍爺的法眼。
You eventually can't flee from the Dharma Eye of the City God.

呃...往後我會好好注意自己的生活和行為。
I will be mindful of my life and behaviour in the future.

很好!
Excellent!

不由人算Not Up To Man 完

138

偶遇福德正神大伯公
A Chance Encounter With The God of Fortune & Virtues

有一天，我欲在年尾主辦一個「年貨一日遊」活動，剛好來到了東部的一間非常有素質的超市。
I wanted to organise a shopping activity for New Year goodies, during the year end. One day, I happened to be at a very high-quality supermarket in the east of Singapore.

那是福德正神大伯公。
真是稀奇啊...
That's the God of Fortune
& Virtues Tua Pek Gong.
How rare…

師父,為什麼稀奇
呢?
Master, why is it
rare?

我從沒在別家超市看到有供奉
神明,而這超市集團我已經看見
了兩間。
I've never seen other supermarkets
enshrine a deity, but for this
supermarket chain, I've already
spotted 2 branches doing so.

唯一遺憾是,這神位的風水
安法有欠妥當,
Only regret is that this altar
Feng Shui is not done right.

會有人事和遠景的問題,
也會影響營業額的彈升。
This will cause interpersonal
and prospect problems, and
also affect revenue.

偶遇大伯公 A Chance Encounter With The God of Fortune & Virtues 完

當心被鬼吃了 Don't Get Eaten By The Ghosts!

時至今日，談鬼依然使人色變。
Even in this modern age, talking about ghosts still instills fear in people.

師父，昨天我和朋友看二部鬼片，
Master, yesterday my friend and I watched 2 horror movies.

這二部電影真是恐怖又好看！
They were really horrifying and great to watch!

這...其實是看完電影後，晚上就怕到睡不著覺了。
Eh, because after watching the movie, I was too scared to sleep at night.

是嗎？妳的精神看起來不太好...
Is it? You don't look well...

師父，上回您不是有來我家看風水嗎？
Master, didn't you come to my house for a Feng Shui audit?

那您有沒有看到我家有鬼呀？
Did you spot any ghost in my home?

還有這裡有沒有鬼在呀？
And are there any ghosts here?

鬼神是佈滿十方法界的,鬼類和人類是沒有多大分別的。

Spirits are everywhere in the ten realms of existence. There isn't much difference between humans and ghosts.

唯一的分別是,鬼類已脫離了肉身,而人類還未脫離肉身。

The only difference lies in ghosts have left their human bodies, while humans have not.

鬼類屬低級靈，只要一個咒語、一個想念，就能攝招衪們來。
Ghosts belong to lowly beings, and can be easily summoned with a mantra or a thought.

就因如此，那些常圖非份的人，鋌而走險的請鬼、養鬼，好逸惡勞的想要不勞而獲。

Thus, people with wayward intent, take huge risk to invite and make offerings to ghosts, so as to reap without sowing.

或許這些「歹徒」並不十分清楚，他們所請所養的鬼，是和他們一樣，貪念甚重的，且法力也會增長，會有不受約束的一天。

Maybe they are unclear that the ghosts they invoke and adopt are like them. The ghosts have insatiable greed, and as their powers grow, they'll be unconstrained one day.

若法力與符力不夠，他們會被反噬。
If the powers and talismans are weak,
the owners get devoured instead.

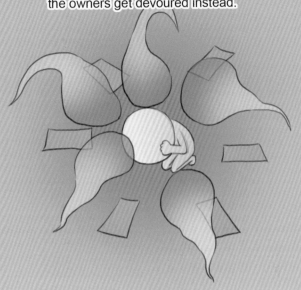

啊...好恐怖。
真的會有人這麼做嗎？
Ah, so scary.
Will there really be people
like that?

也曾有婦女欲請吾去其
住宅捉鬼及收鬼。
Once, a female client invited
me to her house for
ghost-busting.

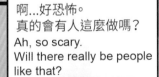

有，過去吾是有幫人處理
被鬼類干擾之事。
There is. I had helped people
with spiritual disturbances in
the past.

好厲害喔！
That's impressive!

其實當時吾是有打算，去「會一會」她宅中的「小朋友」，
Initially, I did intend to go meet the "little friend" in her home,

可惜她接二連三的「做奸犯科」，
But unfortunately, she continuously committed wrongs.

更何況，她先生不相信吾的能力，所以也沒來請吾，此謂因緣不足也。
Moreover, her husband didn't seek my help as he didn't believe in my abilities. This is a lack of affinity.

夫婦倆的起心動念，倒是合了「鬼性」，
The couple's thoughts and intentions match the ghost nature,

是問吾如何捉得完，收得完？
How could I succeed in catching and driving the ghosts?

有可能他們目前宅中的鬼，會幫他們阻止其他鬼進來也說不一定！

Who knows, this ghost in their home may help prevent other spirits from intruding their house!

哈哈哈！
Ha ha ha!

師父，我要如何防範那些鬼跟著我呢？

Master, how do I guard against those ghosts from following me?

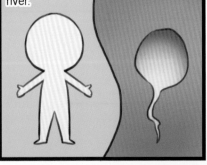

鬼類與人類本來就有界限的。有如井水不犯河水。

There is a boundary between humans and spirits, just like water in the well does not cross the path of water in the river.

但因妳用法術去攝招祂們來，從此祂們就一直跟著自己。

But if you use magic arts to invoke the ghosts, they will follow you from then on.

再加上差遣祂們去辦的事，皆屬惡行的話，

If you dispatch the ghosts to help you in wrongdoings.

自己身上的鬼氣會越來越重，最終將輪迴到鬼處。

The ghostly energy on you will intensify, and eventually you'll be reborn in the ghost realm.

拜師又叛師，起心動念皆不敬師、受人恩惠不圖報、貪得無厭、
Behaviour like betrayal and disrespect towards your master in your thoughts, not recompensing your benefactors, insatiable greed,

喜佔他人便宜、辱罵佛菩薩神明等等，
liking to take advantage of others, insulting gods, Buddhas and Bodhisattvas etc,

這樣的人，鬼就每天愛他多一些。
will only make the ghosts "love" you more!

那如何做才不會讓鬼喜歡自己，不會鬼被吃呢？
Then what should I do so that ghosts will not like me and devour me?

我，日寫夜也寫，以文章的慧光照你們，
I write relentlessly day and night, for my essays to radiate the light of wisdom on all of you,

希望你們正心正念，那就不用當心被鬼吃了。
hoping that they inspire proper and wholesome thinking in you. Then you need not worry being devoured by the ghosts.

要借助鬼眾來幫自己獲得人世間的奢求時，
要特別想清楚。

Please think carefully if you
wish to enlist the help of ghosts
for your worldly material gains.

妳養一個靈，那個靈是無形的，
他幾時變妳都不知道，

When you adopt a ghost, who is
formless, you've no idea when he
changes.

他們始終有無止盡的貪念，
They have insatiable greed
and desires.

而現實生活中的人與事，妳大概還可以預測得到，
但妳不知道鬼變化多端啊！

You can still somewhat predict for people and matters in real life,
but with these invisible spirits, you never know of their changes!

所以要借助鬼通的人務必要思考，再思考。
So, for those of you wanting ghostly help,
think over it again and again.

謝謝師父的開導，
我明白了。
Thank you Master for your
guidance.I understand.

當心被鬼吃了
Don't Get Eaten By The Ghosts! 完

兩個被世俗人「尊崇」的節日，都不約而同的在年關將近。

There are two festivals at year end that are widely celebrated by the world.

這時候，一批又一批的「紅男綠女」，
「濃妝搖滾」的相約出外狂歡，

At that time, hordes after hordes of merry-making men and women, decked in festive clothes and makeup, will throng the streets to party.

有的「忘情森巴舞」，有的「酒醉的Tango」、有的「花言巧語」，等等。

Some take to "senseless samba", others prefer "drunken tango", while the rest engage in "sweet talking"

當然，這些「紅男綠女」，是不甚明白他們為何，
不能也不該這麼做的。

Naturally, these men and women do not understand why they cannot and should not do what they are doing.

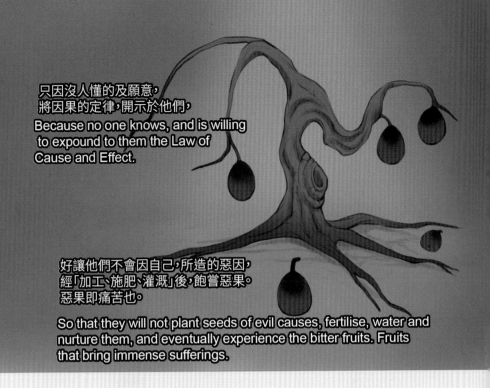

只因沒人懂的及願意，
將因果的定律，開示於他們，
Because no one knows, and is willing
to expound to them the Law of
Cause and Effect.

好讓他們不會因自己，所造的惡因，
經「加工、施肥、灌溉」後，飽嘗惡果。
惡果即痛苦也。
So that they will not plant seeds of evil causes, fertilise, water and
nurture them, and eventually experience the bitter fruits. Fruits
that bring immense sufferings.

一時的快樂，換來永恆的悲哀，
這肯定不是有智慧的人。

Enjoying a fleeting moment
of pleasure, in exchange for
an eternity of sorrow, is
certainly not typical of a wise
person.

我懷孕了...
I'm pregnant…

是我們那晚喝醉
時懷上的....
It's from that night
when we got drunk…

怎麼辦？
Now what?

我根本沒有錢養
孩子啊...
I don't have
money to raise a
child…

因為，真正有智慧的人，
絕不會在因果裡。

Because a genuinely wise person will never trap himself in karma.

因果/Karma

也就是不在因果中，才是也
才能永久無苦安樂。
懂嗎？會嗎？

And because he's not within karma, he will and can enjoy eternal bliss with no suffering.
Do you understand?
Do you know how?

欲望大多是敗德的，而敗了德，一切的祈願與希望，都將落空
及更生障礙。

Most desires are non-virtuous. When virtues get compromised, all prayers and hopes will come to nothing, and obstacles shall arise.

那些什麼幸福、什麼快樂、什麼美滿的，也將是遙不可及的「夢想」罷了，永遠不會出現在你們的生命裡。

Whatever bliss, happiness and joy you crave for will become an unattainable dream, never manifesting in your life.

吾，玳瑚師父，為何如此的快樂自在，原因及秘訣就在吾的每日修行，吾每日的修行都在清除欲望啊！

Why can I, Master Dai Hu, live so joyfully and at ease? The reason & secret lie in my daily spiritual practice, which cleanses me of my worldly desires!

當我們早上起床，望向窗外的無雲晴空時，心中知曉今天是好天氣。
當我們事事都如意的時候，我們知曉，這陣子的我們，還在當旺的氣運中。

When we rise in the morning, and look out of the window to see a clear blue sky greet us, we know in our hearts that it will be fine weather today.
When we are on a roll, with everything going our way, we know that we are still in a prosperous luck period.

當我們見到自己的親屬、眷屬或友人在病床上，我們知曉她他們正在氣衰時。

When we see our family, relatives or friends on the sick bed, we know that their luck energy is on the slide.

我們由此明白，氣足運盛，氣衰運弱的道理，時時保持氣足，而不是時時泄氣及漏氣啊！

Thus, we can understand the principle - the fuller our Qi (energy essence) the more prosperous our luck. The weaker our Qi, the poorer our luck. Our Qi must always be maintained at ample levels, and not constantly let it leak and slip away!

千萬不要以為精盡人才亡。
氣盡人亦亡。

Please do not be mistaken that a person dies only when his life essence(semen) depletes fully. When his Qi is depleted, he bids this world farewell too.

精氣是連著的，是一不是二。

Our life essence and Qi are connected, and must be viewed as a whole.

吾，玳瑚師父父，告訴妳你什麼時候，妳你在泄氣及漏氣。

Let me share with you the various situations when your Qi leaks and slips out of you.

當你在運動、在睡覺、在大小號、在做白日夢、夜間夢、在憂愁、在跳舞、在行房、在狂歡、在捉狂、在玩樂、在胡思亂想、在埋怨、在傷感...，都是在泄氣及漏氣。

When you are exercising, sleeping, excreting or urinating, daydreaming, night dreaming, worrying, dancing, having sexual activity, partying, throwing a fit, having fun, thinking nonsense, complaining, feeling sad, etc, your Qi is being drained.

唯當妳你在修法，誦經持咒、或說法時，才不在泄氣及漏氣中。

Only when you are doing your spiritual practice, reciting the sutra, chanting the mantra, or expounding the Dharma, is your Qi being preserved.

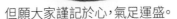

但願大家謹記於心，氣足運盛。

May everyone remember this well, and enjoy an abundance of Qi and a prosperous fortune.

氣足運盛 The Fortune Prospers When The Qi Is Full 完

快樂的本源即是戒　Happiness Originates from Precepts

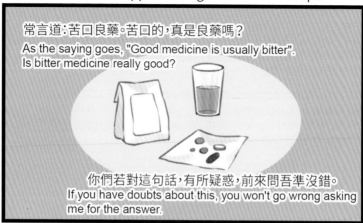

常言道：苦口良藥。苦口的，真是良藥嗎？
As the saying goes, "Good medicine is usually bitter".
Is bitter medicine really good?

你們若對這句話，有所疑惑，前來問吾準沒錯。
If you have doubts about this, you won't go wrong asking me for the answer.

吾，玳瑚師父，是研習佛法及玄學多年的師父。
現在就為你們排憂解惑。
I am a Master who had researched and studied Dharma and Chinese
Metaphysics for many years. Let me now
resolve your woes and answer your question.

宇宙的真理是平等、平衡。套一句簡單的話，即是恰到好處。
The truth of the Universe is equality and balance. To put it simply,
that means just right.

這句「恰到好處」再簡單一點，即是不多不少剛剛好也。

故太苦則傷心，太甜則傷胰，太鹹則傷腎，太酸則傷胃……。

In even simpler terms, that means not too much, not too little, just hitting the right spot.

If it is too bitter, the heart will be depleted. Too sweet, the spleen will be injured. Too salty, your kidneys will be hurt. Too sour, your stomach will suffer.

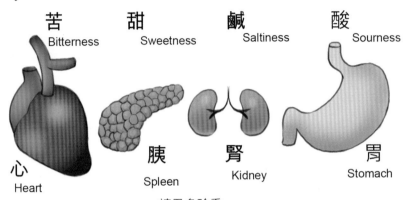

苦　　Bitterness
甜　　Sweetness
鹹　　Saltiness
酸　　Sourness
心　　Heart
胰　　Spleen
腎　　Kidney
胃　　Stomach

請君多珍重。

So please keep well, my dear readers.

很少很少人會願意挨苦、吃苦的，這是平常的。

Very few people are willing to endure hardship and suffer. That is normal.

但問題是，你們雖不想挨苦、吃苦，可是卻又活得越久，
越老越辛苦，甚至是痛苦。

Problem is, while you don't wish to suffer, life is bound to be tougher as you live longer and age, even bringing with it pain and distress.

這到底是怎麼一回事？

What is happening?

有些人歸咎於命，有些人歸咎於父母，有些人歸咎於伴侶，
有些人歸咎於⋯⋯。

Some said it is just their lot in life. Some blamed their parents and spouse, and some…

都是爸爸偏心，把錢全給弟弟，
所以才無法送我去國外讀書！

It's all Dad's fault for being bias and giving all the money to younger brother, hence he can't send me overseas to study!

一定是我和你結婚的關係，
我才沒有加薪！

Must be because I married you, so I didn't get any pay increment!

又來了⋯

There she goes again…

其實啊！與其你們在那兒，浪費時光地歸咎來歸咎去，
倒不如發奮圖強，力爭上游的向真正的能者討教成功之道，
或立命之學，這樣才不愧對自己的生命呀！

Truth is, rather than wasting time pointing fingers, you will do better if you buck up and strive to seek advice from a genuinely able man on the formula to success or the way to create your own destiny. Only then, you would not have lived in vain!

難道你們生是苦，死也要苦嗎？
在生前沒累積善功德，死後就到幽冥界受苦啊！
為何這麼笨？

Do you want to suffer your entire life, from birth to death? If there are no merits or virtues accumulated while alive, after your death, you will end up suffering in the Netherworld. Why will you be so foolish?

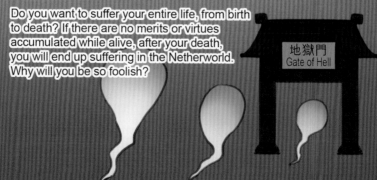

地獄門
Gate of Hell

根據吾多年的探討，人為何越活越辛苦或痛苦，
According to my years of exploration, the main reasons for Man's growing suffering and pain in life

皆離不開「智」與「德」。
boils down to two things: Wisdom and Virtues.

因無智慧故，起心動念皆成障礙。
When one has no wisdom, his every intention and thought become his obstacles.

障礙什麼？
Obstacles to what?

障礙入世之妻、財、子、祿。
Obstacles to worldly pursuits of spouse, wealth, descendants and status.

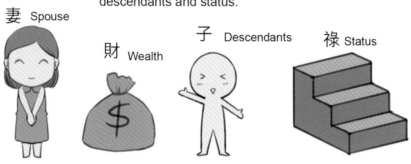

妻 Spouse

財 Wealth

子 Descendants

祿 Status

障礙出世的成就佛果。
Obstacles to spiritual aspirations of attaining Buddhahood.

因無福德與功德故，入世出世皆障礙也。
Due to the absence of virtues and merits, one's path in life, be it secular or spiritual, will be fraught with obstacles.

159

智慧絕非一般的聰明，所以才有「聰明反被聰明誤」，
這句俗話也。
Wisdom is not merely being clever, thus the saying:
Clever people can end up being victims of their own
cleverness.

智慧者，乃能圓滿無礙的觀破，及成就成辦一切事。
A wise person can attain an unimpeded penetrative view
and is able to accomplish all pursuits.

福德、功德具足者，能成就無上道，能賜福賜吉祥給一切眾生。
The person who accumulates sufficient good fortune, merits and
virtues shall attain unsurpassed spiritual accomplishment, and
be able to bestow fortune and auspiciousness to all sentient beings,

令一切眾生所求皆得圓滿。偉哉，勝哉！
allowing them to fulfil their wishes. What a great
and magnificent achievement!

福
Good fortune

吉
Auspiciousness

吉
Auspiciousness

福
Good fortune

咱們尊貴、慈悲、偉大的大聖佛陀，早在兩千六百多年前，
已教導我們戒力多殊勝偉大。
Our esteemed, noble and compassionate Lord Buddha had already taught us, 2600 years ago, the magnificence and nobility of upholding precepts

祂教導我們守戒才能生定，定中才能生慧。
He taught us that only with adherence to precepts, can one's meditative stillness arise, and subsequently, one's wisdom develops.

這也是所有佛教徒畢生的功課，
謂之三無漏學。
This is the lifelong homework of all Buddhists, known as the Threefold Non-Leakage Training.

天道
Heaven Realm

阿修羅道
Asura Realm

人道
Human Realm

Hungry Ghost Realm
餓鬼道

Animal Realm
畜生道

地獄道
Hell Realm

吾等若不依此正法修持，
六道輪迴難逃唉！
蓋有漏皆墮。

If we do not cultivate according to this genuine Dharma, we will not escape from the six realms of reincarnation, for all leakages lead to falls.

結了婚，不守夫道婦道，風月場所流連忘返，紅杏出牆，與同事亂搞愛時，等等。

When a married person does not adhere to marriage rules, lingers at red-light districts, cheats on the spouse or has an affair with a colleague etc.

都是因為不守戒，無定亦無慧。

This is due to failure to uphold the precepts, thus there is no meditative stillness and wisdom.

最後得個婚姻失敗、家庭破裂、爭奪子女扶養權、贍養費等問題。

All these end in a problematic state of failed marriage, broken family, fighting for children custody and alimonies, etc.

我們走！
Let's go!

媽媽...
Mummy…

孩子...
My child…

試問，要多久才能釋懷，才能重回以往的快樂？

Ask yourself, how long must you suffer before happy days return?

所以玳瑚師父告知妳你，快樂的本源即是戒。

This is why Master Dai Hi tells you that precepts is the source of all happiness.

戒
Precepts

快樂的本源即是戒 Happiness Originates from Precepts 完

天下有賊 Thieves Abound In The World

你若是吾標準粉絲的話，
定知曉吾很喜歡詩與偈。

If you're my ardent fan, you'll certainly know that I like poetry and verses very much.

詩是唐代的詩，
偈是佛或古德的偈。

Poetry from the Tang Dynasty, and verses from the Buddha and wise sages.

這一世最早認識唐朝，是在小學時期。

I learned about the Tang Dynasty in my primary school days

當老師告訴我們，在中國唐朝時代，可以說家家戶戶，夜晚就寢時，
不關門也無需擔心賊人入宅，聽了內心讚歎唐朝，不愧為盛世，治安果然好。

My teacher told us that families in those days slept in peace at night, with
no worry of burglar breaking into their homes, even with their doors unlocked.
When I heard that, I was full of awe and praise for the Tang Dynasty.
It deserved to be a time of prosperity with such good public security.

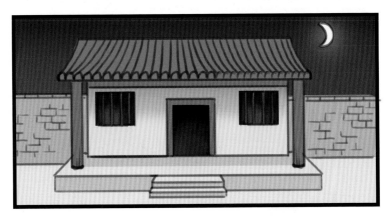

這朝代也蘊育出，享譽中外的大詩人及大修行家，如：玄奘、善無畏、慧果、杜甫、李白、白居易、李商隱。

Many great poets and spiritual practitioners also emerged from this period of time.Great names like Xuan Zhuang, Shan Wu Wei, Hui Guo, Du Pu, Li Bai, Bai Ju Yi, Li Shang Yin, etc.

這裡講個笑話「供養」諸位，一來笑一笑，少一少，二來牽引諸位，進入智慧庫裡，取得離苦得樂的慧寶。

Let me offer a joke to everyone.Firstly, to get you to laugh to stay young at heart. Secondly, to lead everyone into the treasure trove of wisdom to obtain the precious wisdom, that can set you free from endless sufferings and gain you eternal bliss.

有位男子命終墮落幽冥地府，閻羅王審問堂下的男魂—

A man died and his spirit fell into the Netherworld. The King of Hades interrogated him.

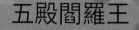

五殿閻羅王

5th Court of Hell : King of Hades

你生前在陽間做何事業？

What was your profession when you were alive?

閻羅王，求您放過我吧！

King of Hades, I beg you to let me go!

我是幫人搬家的！

I help people to move houses!

我幫忙搬家都是不拿錢的！

I don't charge money for helping with the home-moving!

不拿酬款嗎？

You don't charge anything?

你這是善業啊！

This is a good deed of yours!

是的是的！

Yes yes!

口說無憑，來看業鏡吧！

Words alone are no proof. Let's look at the karma mirror!

這面業鏡可是能清清楚楚的照出你生前所做的一切。

This karma mirror can clearly show all that you have done when you were alive

不管是善事還是壞事，全都會顯示出來。

Whether good or bad deeds, everything will be displayed.

來，開始吧！

Come, let's begin!

這...

This…

結果這面業鏡將他的一生都照出來。而他所說的搬家....

In the end, this karma mirror revealed his entire life. The house-moving he was talking about…

太棒了！
偷到許多寶貝！

Awesome! I've stolen many treasures!

今夜又是大豐收！

It's another bountiful harvest tonight!

原來你說不拿錢是這意思啊？

So this is what you mean by not charging money?

你趁人們不在家時，夜裡入屋，搬走他人的財物....

You sneaked into people's homes at night when they were out and moved their valuables away…

對不起！請原諒我這個小賊！

Sorry! Please forgive me this little thief!

賊就是賊。來人，送他去受刑！

A thief is a thief. Men, send him for his punishment!

事實上這人間還是有賊的，所以到處都在張貼海報，或其他相關通告，在新加坡，有很多商場會有個站立的紙皮警察，提醒人們偷盜是犯法的。

Fact is, thieves still exist in this world. Thus you see anti-crime posters and relevant notices everywhere. In Singapore, many shopping centres have this cardboard policeman standee, reminding people that shoplifting is a crime

且近年的超級市場，也雇請多名保安人員，若無賊的話，何必增加此開銷呢？

Also, in recent years, supermarkets are employing more security personnel. If there is no thief, why these extra expenses?

SHOP THEFT IS A
CRIME

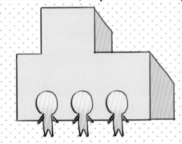

賊的特性是趁人之危的，他們皆在你不注意，
Thieves tend to capitalise on another person's perilous situation. When you are least aware,

你不留意下，行偷盜之事。
and not mindful, they sneak in for a steal

以上所提的賊，是一般人可捕捉得到的。
This kind of thief can usually be apprehended.

接下來所要提到的，是非一般人所不能預防，及捕捉得到的。
Another kind of thief, however, is harder for most people to defend against, much less get apprehended.

唯有真心誠意地實修佛法，方能逃出其魔掌，永得無苦安樂。
Only when you practice the Dharma wholeheartedly can you escape from its evil clutches, and enjoy eternal bliss with no sufferings

佛法中提到的六根，即眼、耳、鼻、舌、身、意，又名六賊。
為何稱為六賊？

In Buddhism, there are the six sense bases, namely the eyes, ears, nose,
tongue, body and mind. They are also known as the six thieves. Why so?

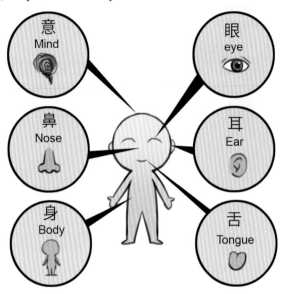

吾說過賊是趁人之危的。

I had said that a thief would pounce during your most perilous.

這六根應無「防護之力」，即好逸惡勞，貪看，
貪聞，貪嗅，貪食，貪是非，貪觸，貪想念，等等，
因而失去人身，甚至萬劫不復啊！

These six sense bases are defenceless and
hence,adverse to labour but
fond of enjoyment. They are
greedy for sight, sound,
smell, food, gossip, touch
and thought, etc,
causing you to lose
your human form, and
be beyond redemption!

這種賊所盜取的，是我們身心與慧命，遠遠，大大地慘重過，
世間的那些身外之物啊！

What these thieves are robbing are our bodies, minds and spiritual lives.
This is far more grievous than those material possessions!

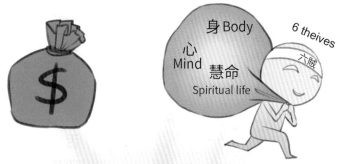

告訴大家，這種賊最怕佛法。
想要天下無賊，唯有佛法。
若無佛法，天下有賊。

Let me tell you, such thieves are most terrified of the Dharma.If you
wish for a world without thieves, only the Dharma can make it happen.
Without the Dharma, the world will be infested with thieves.

天下有賊 Thieves Abound In The World 完

近期有一位少婦來找吾。
A young married woman came to learn the Dharma from me.

她一來，吾就看出她愚痴很重，撒謊成性，也非善良的孩子。

The moment she came, I could see she was very ignorant, a habitual liar and not a kind-hearted child.

師父，我想跟您學佛。

Master, I wish to learn Buddhism from you.

吾沒第一時間說出吾的看見，因為吾一直希望眾生學好。

I didn't immediately say out what I saw, for I always hope that sentient beings will learn well.

師父，我星期六要去做義工了！

Master, I'm going for volunteer work on Saturday!

這是好事。
This is a good thing…

那慈善團體每日準備大約5000份的飯菜，

That charity prepares 5000 meals daily

並送到新加坡有需要的人家中。

and distributes to needy families all over Singapore.

跟您學後，我想多行善！

After learning from you, I wish to do more good!

星期六早上
Saturday morning

唉呀！下雨了，
不去做義工了。
Ah, it's raining!
Not going to
volunteer then.

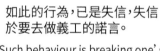

Continue sleeping!
繼續睡覺！

如此的行為，已是失信，失信
於要去做義工的諾言。
Such behaviour is breaking one's
promise. She went back on her
word to volunteer.

這是很嚴重的過失，
This is a very serious fault.

因為她沒有去，就會少一個
人去貢獻給那些需要幫助
的人。
Because of her absence,
there is one less person to
contribute to the needy.

這個過失牽涉到別人，那些本應得到她的救援而沒得到的人。
如果說有十個人等她的話，就會有十次的過失。

This fault implicated other people, the people that needed her help but did not received it. If there were 10 needy people that day waiting for her, her misdeed is multiplied by 10 times.

失約之後，她來找吾學佛...
After her no-show, she came for her Dharma lessons...

師父，對不起，那天我沒到場。
Master, sorry I didn't make it that day.

我下次不會再犯了。
I won't make the same mistake again.

妳要學會守戒，像是不可以飲酒...
You must learn to observe the precepts, like abstaining from alcohol.

這...
This…

明天飲酒會，妳要來喔！
Tomorrow is the drinking session. You must come!

業務小姐！
Miss Operations!

ok!

......

師父，對不起喔！
Master, so sorry!

剛才不是說不能飲酒嗎？
Didn't I just said not to drink alcohol?

抱歉！Sorry!

因為同事邀約的，下回我一定會遵守！
Because my colleague invited me. Next time, I will listen to you!

她跟吾學佛的這四個月來，

In the past 4 months of learning Buddhism from me,

她天天都播電話和發簡訊要求吾讓她回來學佛。

she would call and text me everyday, asking for a chance to resume learning the Dharma from me.

吾每次都給她回來學佛，

I relented every time,

而她每次當下又犯戒律了。

only to see her flout the precepts again.

舉一個很嚴重的例子—
Here's one serious incident:

師父，我公公生日快到了，
Master, my father-in-law's birthday coming.

某天—
One day

是嗎？
那妳要注意—
Oh, then you must take note...

吾知道她家翁的八字，就好心，沒收費的交代她—
I knew her father-in-law's birthday details. Out of kindness, at no charge, I advised her...

妳千萬不可給他吃紅雞蛋和江魚仔，
You must not let him eat red eggs and ikan bills

因為會傷害到他的健康。
as these harm his health.

明白了，謝謝師父的指點。
I understand. Thank you Master for your guidance.

隔天，吾還在電話中再次提醒她—
The next day, I reminded her again over the phone.

記得，慶生不要殺生，不要放江魚仔在壽麵的湯中。
Remember not to kill for a birthday celebration. Don't put ikan bilis in the soup of the longevity noodles.

放心師父，我不會的。
Don't worry, Master. I won't.

她的家翁生日過後，
她來找我學佛。

After her father-in-law's
birthday, she came for
her Dharma lessons.

師父，我來學佛了。

Master, I'm here for
Dharma lessons.

......

我上回叮囑妳公公生日的
事，有照做嗎？

Did you follow my advice
about your father-in-law's
birthday?

這...因為我疏忽
了...

This…because I
overlooked…

我看得出妳在
說謊。

I can tell that
you're lying.

真不愧是師父...

You're a real
Master indeed.

我想說加江魚仔比較
好味，不會怎麼樣....

I thought it would taste
better with ikan bills. It
won't do much harm.

這是一件非常可怕的事情，所以告訴大家千萬不要明知故犯，

This is a very horrifying incident, thus I want to tell everyone not to commit a mistake knowingly.

因為這麼做已經在你的未來製造了一個地獄。

Doing so will create a hell for yourself in the future.

那些江魚仔的生命也會寄託在她身上，一直到她能把牠們超渡以後才能夠還淨。

The spirits of those ikan bilis will pin onto her body till she can deliver their spirits, before her sin is purified.

而她蓄意的下江魚仔「毒害」她的家翁，將會使她「毒性攻心」，直接下三惡道去。

Her deliberate harming of her father-in-law with ikan bills will cause the poison to invade her heart. This will directly pull her down to the Three Evil Paths.

這樣子不是學佛，而已經是學魔了。希望這位少婦能夠趕快覺醒，虔心誠意的天天懺悔，直到有懺相，業障才消除。

This is not learning the Dharma but already following the ways of the Mara. I sincerely hope that this young married woman will wake up from her folly soon, wholeheartedly repent for her misdeeds daily. The day signs of repentance show, will be the day her negative karma is fully eradicated.

毒人終毒己 Done by your own poison 完

畜生道的緣起 The Interdependent Origination of the Animal Realm

六道輪輪迴圖，可知曉何謂六道？
You may know about the Wheel of Life diagram, Six Realms of Rebirth, but do you know what are the Six Realms?

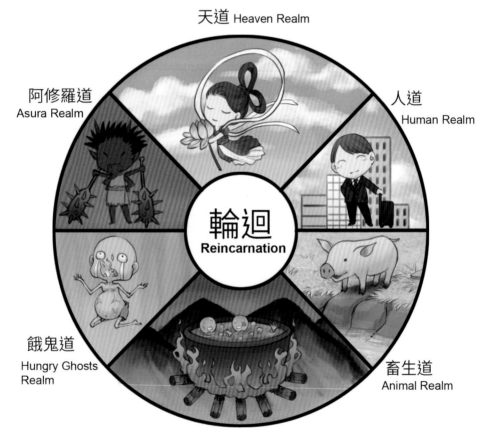

天道 Heaven Realm

阿修羅道
Asura Realm

人道
Human Realm

輪迴
Reincarnation

餓鬼道
Hungry Ghosts
Realm

畜生道
Animal Realm

地獄道 Hell Realm

但要清楚明白六道，天、阿修羅、人、地獄、畜生、餓鬼，各道的緣起，就必需得進一步地實修佛法，以免越修越往六道，甚至三惡道去。那就非常的悲慘嘍！

But to clearly understand the origination of each realm: Devas, Asuras, humans, Hell, animals, and hungry ghosts, you need to level up in your practice of the Dharma, so as not to lose your way and end up in these Six Realms, especially the Three Evil Paths. That will be very disastrous!

多年前，吾還有看電視節目，或閱讀報章時，看到或讀到，某種動物及飛禽等等，將面臨絕種的消息時，心中總有一絲絲的莫明覺受。

Many years back when I still watched the TV or read the papers, I would always feel a tinge of bafflement when I came across news that certain animal species were endangered.

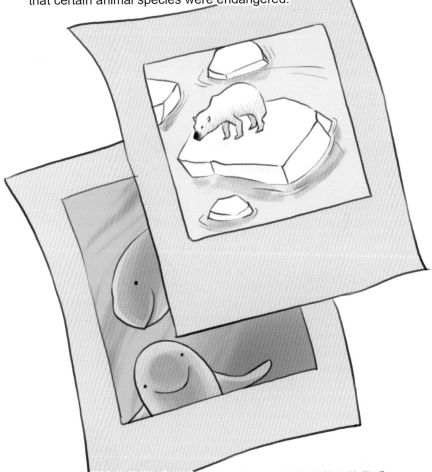

但修習佛法後的吾，有了真實的見地，知曉過去那莫明的覺受，祇是一種無知的一時湧現，而非真實的智慧。

However, after I started the practice of Dharma and attained genuine insight, I realised that those feelings of bafflement were moments of ignorance and not true wisdom.

佛教闡明因與果。緣起緣滅也即是因果。你的心念一起，就是緣起。

The Law of Cause and Effect is clearly explained in Buddhism. The arising and cessation of affinity is also the Law of Cause and Effect. A thought that rises in you marks the beginning of affinity.

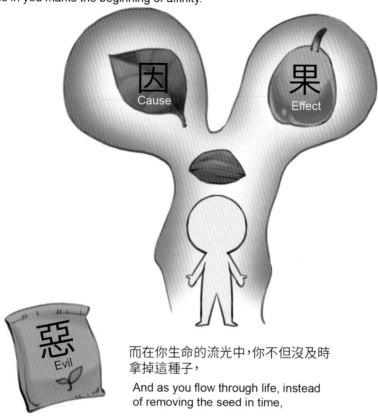

而在你生命的流光中，你不但沒及時拿掉這種子，

And as you flow through life, instead of removing the seed in time,

反而天天「施肥」（惡行為），
不久的將來必得惡果。

you fertilize this seed day after day with your unvirtuous acts, and will surely reap you fruits of retribution in the near future

凡貪、嗔、癡、妒、慢、疑者，都是畜生道的緣起。

因此，某種或任何一種飛禽走獸等等，應該不會這麼快的絕種。

The poisons of greed, hatred, ignorance, jealousy, arrogance and suspicion create the affinity for rebirth in the Animal Realm. Thus, it is highly unlikely that a particular species of animal will go extinct anytime soon.

還記得吾在第28則寫有關一位明知故犯，「下毒」害她家翁的少婦嗎？

那漫畫叫《毒人終毒己》。

Do you remember my 28th article about a married woman who intentionally "poisoned" her father-in-law? That article is titled Done By Your Own Poison.

文中所提的這位少婦，她和她先生曾向吾學習佛法達四個月。
This young married woman, together with her husband, came to learn the Dharma from me for 4 months.

次次來學吾都教導他們，守戒持戒的重要，如佛教基本五戒，以及儒家八德，還有己所不欲，勿施於人，等等。
Without fail, in every lesson, I would teach them the importance of upholding the precepts, such as the 5 Precepts of Buddhism, the 8 Virtues of Confucianism, and not to do unto others what they do not want others do unto them.

恥
sense of shame

孝
filial piety

不殺生
No killing

廉
integrity

悌
sibling harmony

不偷盜
No stealing

不邪淫
No sexual misconduct

義
honour

忠
loyalty

不妄語
No false speech

不飲酒
No taking of intoxicants

禮
propriety

信
trustworthiness

在她家翁生辰的前幾天，吾還特別地接聽她的來電，以確保她清楚知曉，不該放什麼食材，煮麵線給其家翁食。
A few days before her father-in-law's birthday, I specially made time to take her call, just to ensure that she was aware what ingredient to avoid, in the rice noodles she cooked for her father-in-law.

記得，慶生不要殺生，不要放江魚仔在壽麵的湯中。
Remember not to kill for a birthday celebration. Don't put ikan bilis in the soup of the longevity noodles.

放心師父，我不會的。
Don't worry, Master. I won't.

家翁不久前，才從中風康復過來，皮膚生濃剛好，
這些她全然不顧的，狠心明知故犯。

Her father-in-law had just recovered from a stroke and a recent bout of
pus-filled sores on his skin. However, she ignored all these and cruelly
went against my advice.

她這一犯，已爲她的未來打造一個地獄，也有了畜生道的緣起。
她「幹了案」之後，吾有再接見她多一次。

Her wilful action has created a realm of Hell for her future and planted
an affinity for rebirth in the Animal Realm. I met her again after she
committed the "crime"

那一次的接見，她身上已有了一團業氣，而這業氣（毒氣），
也已出現在她的臉上（毒瘡）。

During that meeting, an aura of negative karmic energy had
enveloped her body and manifested on her face as an infected
acne.

若不快力行懺悔，毒氣（業氣）
攻心，三惡道哪裡逃啊！
這就是毒人終毒己的慘報。

If she does not seek repentance
fast, the negative karmic energy
shall penetrate her heart and
there will be no escape from the
Three Evil Paths! This is the
tragic ending of a venomous
person falling to her own poison.

畜生道的緣起 The Interdependent Origination of the Animal Realm 完

拜天公 Paying Homage to The Jade Emperor

春節間的正月初九，就是中天玉皇大天尊的聖誕。
During the Spring Festival, the 9th day of the 1st Lunar month marks the holy birthday of the Supreme Jade Emperor.

兒時，每當這偉大節日到來時，吾很自然、很直接的感應一股非常強盛、非常祥瑞、非常喜慶的磁波，從十方湧現。

When I was a kid, I always felt a very strong wave of immensely, auspicious and joyous energies surging in from ten directions, as this great festival drew closer.

家父家母家姊們，在這一年一度的「聖誕節」，可說是從早忙到晚。

My parents and elder sisters would be busy from dawn till dusk, preparing for this annual celebration.

吾則白天幫忙摺金紙，夜晚幫忙端供品及其他，之後就躲進臥房裡，暫且不敢再到客廳「阻礙交通」，更何況家父做起事來，一向都很「認真」的。

I would help fold the joss paper in the day, and prepare the offerings at night.
Then, I would hide in my room so as not to "obstruct traffic" in the living room.
Moreover, my father was a very serious man in such matters.

吾，玳瑚師父，這一世的「示現」，就是要以修證的光明，照亮你們，讓你們「暗處逢生」，絕望中生起希望，且還得引領你們「離苦得樂」。

My existence this life is to shine the Light of Attainment upon you, so that you will find hope amidst the darkness, and lead you towards the cessation of sufferings and enjoyment of bliss.

因此，才寫作這麼多的文章，辦餐會與茶會，啟開你們的智慧呀！

That is why I have been writing endlessly, and holding learning sessions to open up your innate wisdom!

光明與智慧是同體的。

Light and wisdom are of the same body

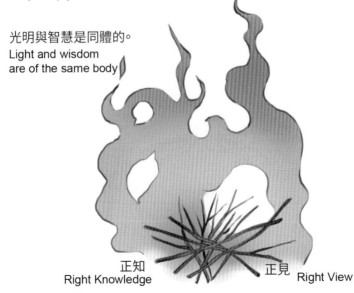

正知
Right Knowledge

正見
Right View

而光明產生之前，一定要有柴薪，這些柴薪即是正知正見也。

To ignite the fire of Light, one will need firewood and this firewood are Right Knowledge and Right View.

正知正見的反意詞，當然就是邪知邪見。
The opposite of these will of course be Evil Knowledge and Evil View.

你為何快樂不起來，皆因你缺乏正知正見啊！
The reason for your unhappiness is the lack of Right
Knowledge and Right View!

 Evil Knowledge Evil View

很多很多人，都是「亂拜一通的」。
也確實有為數不少之人，毫無拜拜的信仰。
Many people are doing prayers haphazardly and a considerable number
of people do not believe in praying.

或許你們想要知道，兩者之間，誰對誰錯。答案是兩者皆錯。
You may wish to know, of these 2 groups, who is right and who is wrong?
My answer: Both are wrong.

先說「亂拜一通的」這一群吧！
Let's talk about the group who prays haphazardly.

他們雖亂拜，起碼他們有拜，
正所謂有拜有保祐啊！

They may be doing it wrongly,
but at the very least, they do
pray. As the saying goes, as
long as you pray, you shall
be protected!

祇是他們路子走錯了而已，
只要稍加指導與指引，日後
也就漸漸「不亂拜」了。

It is just that they took the wrong
path, but with some guidance,
they will not be praying haphazardly
in the future.

至於毫無拜拜信仰的這一群，大多屬於「自我」意識較重者，也就是傲慢。
As for the other group who does not pray at all, they are mostly more
ego-conscious. In other words, arrogant.

這群人就完全失去，超越命運的能力與助力，
實為可悲也。

These people have completely lost the ability and help to overcome
their destinies. It is really a pity.

南無天公玉皇大天尊，有如吾等有情眾生之父，對吾等疼愛有加，所以才會有「上天有好生之德」，這句話呀！

The Heavenly Supreme Jade Emperor is like the father of all sentient beings, showering us with love and compassion, thus the saying "Heaven cares for every living being"!

既然是父親，祂的聖誕獻上我們爲人子女的，誠意供品與賀詞，乃是理所當然的哦！

Since He is like a father to us, it is only right that we, as His children, sincerely offer our wishes and offerings to Him on His holy birthday.

若你往年「成績」，不是很理想，你可以恭恭敬敬的，向祂懺悔，
並祈求祂加持與庇佑，讓你來年修得更好、做得更好，

If you have not been doing well in the past years, now is the time
to respectfully seek repentance from Him, and pray
for His blessings and protection, so that your spiritual practice and
career will improve in the next year.

這才是拜天公真正的內涵與素養，謂之為正信，而非迷信。

This is the real meaning and purpose of paying homage to the
ruler of Heaven. Such is the right belief and not confused belief.

人生的妻、財、子、祿、壽，祂自然會給於賜福。

He will naturally endow you with worldly blessings of a spouse,
wealth, descendants, status and longevity.

拜天公 Paying Homage to The Jade Emperor 完

國家圖書館出版品預行編目資料

向善向上2／玳瑚師父著. --初版.--臺中市：白
象文化，2018.12
　　面；　公分
ISBN 978-986-358-765-1（第2冊：平裝）

224.517　　　　　　　　　　107020791

向善向上2
Towards Kindness, Towards Betterment 2

作　　者　玳瑚師父
漫　　畫　張英
英文翻譯　李季謙、黃騰慶
校　　對　李季謙
發 行 人　張輝潭
出版發行　白象文化事業有限公司
　　　　　412台中市大里區科技路1號8樓之2（台中軟體園區）
　　　　　出版專線：（04）2496-5995　　傳眞：（04）2496-9901
　　　　　401台中市東區和平街228巷44號（經銷部）
　　　　　購書專線：（04）2220-8589　　傳眞：（04）2220-8505
專案主編　徐錦淳
出版編印　林榮威、陳逸儒、黃麗穎、水邊、陳婷婷、李婕
設計創意　張禮南、何佳誼
經紀企劃　張輝潭、徐錦淳、廖書湘
經銷推廣　李莉吟、莊博亞、劉育姍、林政泓
行銷宣傳　黃姿虹、沈若瑜
營運管理　林金郎、曾千熏
印　　刷　基盛印刷工場
初版一刷　2018年12月
初版二刷　2020年6月
初版三刷　2022年7月
初版四刷　2024年2月
定　　價　400元

白象文化　印書小舖　出版‧經銷‧宣傳‧設計
www.ElephantWhite.com.tw　PressStore出版經銷
f 自費出版的領導者　購書 白象文化生活館